A Video Game Story
Dan Ashcraft

©2020

Download the Audio Version of A Video Game Story 1 FREE

If you love listening to audio books on-the-go, I have great news for you. You can download the audio book version of this book for **FREE** just by signing up for a **FREE** 30-day audible trial! See below for more details!

Audible trial benefits

As an audible customer, you'll receive the below benefits with you 30-day free trial:

- Free audible copy of this book

- After the trial, you will get 1 credit each month to use on any audiobook

- Your credits automatically roll over to the next month if you don't use them

- Choose from over 400,000 titles

- Listen anywhere with the audible app across multiple devices

- Make easy, no hassle exchanges of any audiobook you don't love

- Keep your audiobooks forever, even if you cancel your membership

- And much more

Go to the links below to get started
FOR AUDIBLE US

bit.ly/avideogamestory2

FOR AUDIBLE UK

bit.ly/avideogamestory2uk

Free Bonus!

Want to get a FREE 'A Video Game Story: Another Magical Controller?!' Ebook? This is an awesome short story that is a part of the 'A Video Game Story' world!

GO TO THIS LINK FOR YOUR FREE 'A VIDEO GAME STORY' EBOOK! -

bit.ly/avideogamestory

Enjoy!

© Copyright 2020 - All rights reserved.

The content contained within this book may not be reproduced, duplicated or transmitted without direct written permission from the author or the publisher.

Under no circumstances will any blame or legal responsibility be held against the publisher, or author, for any damages, reparation, or monetary loss due to the information contained within this book, either directly or indirectly.

Legal Notice:

This book is copyright protected. It is only for personal use. You cannot amend, distribute, sell, use, quote or paraphrase any part, or the content within this book, without the consent of the author or publisher.

Disclaimer Notice:

Please note the information contained within this document is for educational and entertainment purposes only. All effort has been executed to present accurate, up to date, reliable, complete information. No warranties of any kind are declared or implied. Readers acknowledge that the author is not engaged in the rendering of legal, financial, medical or professional advice. The content within this book has been derived from various sources. Please consult a licensed professional before attempting any techniques outlined in this book.

By reading this document, the reader agrees that under no circumstances is the author responsible for any losses, direct or indirect, that are incurred as a result of the use of the information contained within this document, including, but not limited to, errors, omissions, or inaccuracies.

Hi Gamers, Please Leave A Review On Amazon!

Thank you for reading my book! It really means the world to me. If you enjoy this book, then I'd like to ask you for a favor. Would you be kind enough to leave an honest review on Amazon? It'd be greatly appreciated and help other gamers with their reading skills! I read EVERY review I receive and each one helps me become the best writer I can be!

Have fun!

Dan Ashcraft

Table Of Contents

Free Bonus! 4

Chapter 1: Don't Be Late! 8

Chapter 2: "We're gonna get you, Jason!" 12

Chapter 3: A Window Of Opportunity! 16

Chapter 4: The old, Mysterious Controller 20

Chapter 5: A Superhero Comes To Life 27

Chapter 6: These couldn't be real super powers? 32

Chapter 7: "He Seems To Have Gone Crazy" 38

Chapter 8: "You've Got To Fix The Controller" 43

Chapter 9: Stuck Here Forever 48

Chapter 10: Become Superheroes And Make This World A Better Place 54

Chapter 1: Don't Be Late!

Twelve-year-old Jason Ash was getting ready for school. He woke up from his bed with a groan. He had spent a lot of his time staying up late playing his favorite video game 'Power Wolf Heroes' and did not want to leave the house. He wished he did not ever have to go to school. What was the point of going to school when he would always end up as a victim of a bully? There were three students at Jason's school who were always fond of chasing him and giving him a hard time whenever the day was over. It had happened last week and it had happened the week before. Now today was the beginning of another school week and he was not eager to go, but his mother would not hear of his decision to not attend his classes.

"School has made us successful," Mrs Ash would always say, "and you must be successful too."

Jason was not really close to his parents. They were always busy traveling on various business trips and he was usually left by himself. Once, Jason had tried to skip school. He had played his video games all day instead. The school had called his Mom and she had taken the next available flight back to Nebraska. She had chastised Jason and made him promise not to skip school again.

The time was 6:15am. He figured he could still play Power Wolf Heroes for thirty minutes before getting ready for school. He switched on the TV and the game console. Then he relaxed back and began to play. Of all the games he had played, Power Wolf Heroes was his all-time favorite. The game came on and he selected his character .There were about two dozen characters he could select from but Jason always picked the one he liked best – Nero. This was one of the most powerful characters in the entire game. Nero had the power of creating fire from any part of his body. He could create the fire on his palm and throw it against the enemy or he could turn his entire body into a ball of fire and consume his adversary. Whenever Jason picked Nero, he was rarely defeated. It was like there was a kind of chemistry between the two of them. He always wished he had the kind of power Nero possessed. With that kind of power nobody would ever bully him again. He smiled when he thought about what he would do to Greg, Matt and Anderson whenever they tried to bully him again. He would set a magic fire on their tails, a little magic on them was what they needed and they would scurry away like scared kittens.

But like Nero, having the power was not only for fighting direct enemies too. Nero used his power for justice. Jason would do the same, he would go around the state of Nebraska stopping criminals and handing them over to the police. He would be the hero of Nebraska. People would look up to him for their salvation. There would not be any bully in schools anymore because he would always be there to make them pay. Innocent children who could not defend themselves would be able to go to school without having the fear of being bullied.

As he played the game, he was lost in the world of the game. He wished he could disappear from his own world and appear in the heroes' world. Life would be a lot simpler if he had his own superpowers. Fighting bad people would be so much fun. And from the way he was playing the game, he had no doubt in his mind that he would easily defeat his enemies. He was a natural.

Whenever Jason decided not to use Nero, he would pick Crackle who was another powerful hero. Crackle possessed the power of making thunder crack. Whenever the thunder cracked, a bolt of electricity would descend from the sky and strike the enemies. No matter ow many enemies there were, the thunder would strike them all. Crackle's power reminded Jason of Thor, but where Thor carried a hammer, Crackle carried nothing. Also, crackles eyes did not turn into an element of fire like Thors'. Besides the fact that Crackle could control thunder, he was also a very good fighter. Crackle always fought in a kung fu style and this always excited Jason. The boy wished he was Crackle because he wanted to fight in a kung fu style like the fighting hero.

When it was 7:30, Jason had to force himself to stop playing. The game was an addictive one, and had he not disciplined himself. He would still be playing in the next hour but he didn't want to be late for school. He switched off the television, then the games console, and walked out of his room. His waffles had already been placed on the dining table by the house-help named Mrs Thandie, the woman who had been working for the family long before Jason was born. He quickly devoured his food and ran out of the house to meet the waiting school bus in the street. Every morning by 7:45, the bus would wait outside for five minutes. If Jason did not come out within this time, he would miss it. Then he would either have to go and take the public train to school or he would skip school for that day. Jason had missed the bus twice and he had suffered the consequences. He had been so engrossed in playing Power Wolf Heroes that he did not hear the horn of the bus outside. And because he had promised his mother not to skip school again, he had found his way to school by every means possible. He had walked to the train station and sat beside a dusty old man who continued to cough in Jason's direction, much to the shock of the little boy. And by the time Jason finally got off the train, he did not feel any more clean. The second time, he was lucky. He found a bus going towards his school and he had boarded it. Although it was not an enjoyable ride either, it was a lot better than his experience in the train.

He always liked sitting beside Emily in the bus. Emily was his crush. They were both in the same class but he never got the confidence to tell her that he wanted to be friends. He was scared that she would turn him down. He would not be able to deal with that kind of rejection. He guessed it was best he didn't speak out. At least it was not yet the time to speak his mind. Saying the wrong thing at the wrong moment might have a catastrophic effect on him. He might be the laughing stock of the class. Emily had a close friend whom she told everything to. If she told Linda what he had done, Linda might tell the whole class and he would become the class joke. Being bullied was hard enough to cope with, he wouldn't want to be mocked too.

As he climbed into the school-bus, he found Brian sitting with Emily. He was immediately consumed with a feeling of jealousy.

"Hi Jason," Emily greeted as he passed them by to sit at the other end of the bus.

"Hello Emily," he responded grimly. He tried his best to make sure his emotion was not reflected in his voice. While he responded to Emily's greeting, Brian did not bother looking to his side. Jason was treated as if he didn't exist.

Jason was not fond of Brian. In fact, they were not fond of each other. They always avoided each other at every chance they got. Jason believed Brian had intentionally taken his place beside Emily simply to spite him. Brian wanted him to feel jealous, and his plan was working tremendously. While he sat in the back, he watched Emily and Brian with disapproval. Occasionally, Brian would steal a glance in his direction, give a wicked smile and whisper something into Emily's ear. The girl would smile and then punch Brian lightly in the shoulder. Jason's face was beet red with anger. Everything Brian was saying to Emily was being done intentionally.

Brian must have somehow found out that Jaon liked Emily so he had decided to use that to mess with him. Surely, Brian was not interested in being Emily's friend; he was only doing all these things just to make Jason angry. He had even boldly put his arm on Emily's shoulder, something even Jason himself lacked the confidence to do. And surprisingly, Emily did not push his arm away. Jason was beginning to feel that Emily probably wanted to be friends with Brian. He wondered if there was any chance of him and Emily ever working out.

He wished he had the power of Ransin, one of the characters in Power Wolf Heroes whose ability was reading people's minds. With such a power, he would be able to determine whether Emily liked him as much as he liked her; he would know if she truly liked Brian. He would know those who liked him and those that didn't. He would know everything. He wanted to be a superhero.

While he was thinking about the world of impossibility, someone sat beside him in the car. It was Naomi, Brian's friend in the class.

"Hello Jason. How are you this morning?" she asked him. She seemed strangely interested in him.

"I'm fine, Naomi. How are you?" He was short of any other response to give. This was strange indeed. Naomi had never come to sit with him in the bus before. It was often Naomi and Brian sitting together, everyone knew that, just like they knew he and Emily often sat together in the bus.

But it seemed like Brian had broken that tradition. He had neglected Naomi to go and sit with Emily. Jason suddenly smiled. He now understood what was going on. It wasn't like Naomi was interested in being his friend, obviously. She had come to sit with him just to make Brian jealous as he had made her. Well, it seemed like two could play the game. He warmed up toward Naomi. They didn't really want to be close friends, but they had both agreed to play along.

They began to chat. It was a nice flow between them. For a moment, Jason forgot about Emily. Naomi turned out to be a very interesting girl. He was even telling her about the game he played at home. He invited her to visit him one of these days so that they could play the game together. As he chatted with Naomi, Jason noticed that the proud expression on Brian's face had changed. He was constantly looking toward their direction; Jason loved the turn of events. It seemed like the jealousy had been transferred back to Brian. He didn't seem interested in chatting with Emily anymore; his eyes were fixed on Jason and Naomi. Jason decided to do what Brian had done to Emily; he put his arm on Naomi's shoulder and drew her closer to himself. He could see the expression of blind jealousy in Brian's eyes.

As he threw his elbow on Naomi's shoulder, Emily looked back and saw what was going on. Jason quickly dropped his arm down. He did not seem to understand the expression on Emily's face. He couldn't tell whether she was angry or jealous. Her face was expressionless. He wished she would at least look angry. With that she would know that she was interested in being his friend. This blank expression was really confusing, it was as if Emily didn't care who he chose to play with, and this worried him immensely. If this action was not enough to make her angry, then it meant only one thing; she didn't care about him. She had no iota of friendship feelings for him, and this broke his heart. Suddenly, the zeal to play with Naomi was lost on him. He was moody throughout the rest of the journey to school.

Chapter 2: "We're gonna get you, Jason!"

Jason did not concentrate on the teaching in class. He was once again lost in his world of gaming adventures. He kept thinking about the heroes of his favorite game – Nero, Crackle, Ransin, and others. Playing the game was the only time he found solace. He could play the game all his life as long as he had food available; he would never get tired of playing Power Wolf Heroes. As the teacher continued lecturing the class, Jason became bored so he brought out his sketch pad and began to draw Nero. He had seen him a million times already so he was able to draw the image from his head, putting in every detail about the character. This was not the first time he drew Nero, but this was his first time he drew him in this particular pose; he loved drawing the superhero in various postures.

Jason wanted to become a video game designer. He wanted to design his own kinds of heroes and he had been drawing sketches of many imaginary heroes. He had named a few and their abilities. There was Riski who was so powerful that he could stop a moving train. Evarel was female and she was very fast; she could run at the speed of light. Mentini always danced whenever he fought his enemies. For now he had no idea about making all these characters come to life in a video game but he was going to study the course and bring them to life. People would love his characters just as he loved Nero.

He wanted school to be over so that he could return home and play his game. He could not imagine going a whole day without playing Power Wolf Heroes; he might fall sick from not playing and completing the levels! His mother had said he was addicted to the game and he had disagreed with her, but deep down he knew that he could not do without playing the game. He wished he could have a partner to play the game with, because Power Wolf Heroes allowed multi-playing, but he had no friends to play with. Besides, the game was not a popular one; only a few people could play it. His parents had bought it for him two years ago when he turned ten years old. They had bought it at an old video games store for a very expensive price. The store-keeper had told them that the game was a classic; it had been played by great people for a hundred years; only few people all over the world could play it. The old store-keeper had doubted that their kid would like the game; he had suggested they bought a more modern one but Jason's Mom had stuck with paying for Power Wolf Heroes. She had believed strongly that Jason would enjoy. Her excuse was that the latest games had too much noise and graphics showing monsters and zombies! The Power Wolf Heroes video game was too old to show all that. So they had paid for Power Wolf Heroes and brought it home.

Jason's Dad had thought the boy would be disappointed by the birthday gift. He had wanted to buy a leading brand-new games console for the boy like other parents always did, but his wife had stuck to Power Wolf Heroes. And so he had pushed his wife to present the gift to Jason. To the man's utter surprise, Jason had jumped up in happiness when he opened the box and saw the game. He had fallen in love with it immediately.

He had rushed to his room and connected the game to his TV. For the rest of that day, Jason was busy playing the game and having the best experience of his life.

Everything about the game had been magical to Jason. Although it contained old school graphics, there was something about the game that drew Jason close to it; he felt like he was part of those heroes in the game. Whenever they spoke, he always felt like they spoke directly to him. Each time he played the game, he was transported to another world – a new world, an exciting world of adventure. Whenever he fought with any of the characters, he felt like he was the character.

After a while, Jason began to wonder if there were other people playing this kind of game in other parts of the world. He suddenly wanted to meet them; he wanted to know their experience as they played the game. He wanted to know if there were new tricks he could use in the game. He started searching for other people who played the game. The first thing he did was type in the name of the game in his parents computer. The result came out blank. He had been shocked. How could the computer not recognize this kind of interesting game? He checked the bottom of the console and typed the name of the company that manufactured it; again, the results came out empty again. There was no record of the manufacturing company anywhere!

How could this be? He started wondering. Something didn't seem right. But after a few days of fruitless searching, Jason gave up and continued enjoying the game. As far as he was concerned, he was the only person in the world who played this kind of game. He had even gone to a public gaming arena and asked about Power Wolf Heroes; nobody seemed to have heard about the game before. He was totally confused. Well, he would play it and enjoy himself. This was not the kind of game that deserved to go into extinction; it should be played from generation to generation. It should be the basis of all the modern games of today. But no one thought such a game existed; and if they didn't know of its existence, how would they be able to improve it? But to Jason, the game needed no improvement; it was already perfect as it was.

Jason was so busy working on the sketch of his heroes that he totally forgot that school had closed. Whenever he started drawing, it was like he was playing his game again. He had become oblivious of everything going on in his surroundings. He wouldn't leave until he had perfected everything he was drawing. After an hour he finished the job and returned his pad into his bag and left the class. He was walking in the corridor when he met his greatest enemies; the three bullies he had always tried to avoid. But no matter how much he tried to avoid them, they always found him. He quickly turned around to walk back to where he was coming from but it was too late, they had already seen him.

"Hey Jason," Greg said from afar, "Where are you going, bro?"

Jason did not stop, he kept walking off. He wanted to be as far away from them as possible. He wished he could find a teacher that would protect him from these bullies.

"Stop there, Jason," Matt had called from behind.

But Jason kept walking, increasing his pace. He looked back when he started hearing the shuffling of feet. The three bullies were coming after him. He took to his heels immediately. He turned to his left and followed the long hallway. His pursuers were coming after him with determination. Jason was afraid; he knew what they would do to him if they caught up with him. He had stressed them by making them run and they would make him pay for that. Today's assault would be worse because there was no one around that would save him. The last time, the janitor had stepped in when the boys were harassing him. He had walked away with a few bruises, but this time around, there was no savior in sight. He had to run for safety; he had to save himself. His heart was beating fast!

"We're gonna get you, Jason!" Anderson had called after him.

Jason still continued running. His pursuers were not only bigger than him, they were also older. Each one of them was at least fifteen years old. They had picked Jason as their victim because the boy was everything they would never be. Jason was cheerful, intelligent and from a family that lived on the nicer side of town, while his bullies came from the bad side of town. The first time they had attacked Jason, they had taken his money and beaten him up. Jason could not tell his school teachers for the fear of the bullying getting worse. He also didn't want Emily to know what he was going through. So he had taken every punishment the boys inflicted on him. The victimizations had always been going on week-in and week-out. He had to save himself now; he had to run for safety. He thought about running into a class and locking himself in it, but that would not be a great idea. The boys would find a way to get the door open. The only thing he could do was continue running, hoping that the boys would grow tired of him and stop pursuing. But it didn't seem likely at the moment. They were determined to catch up with him. Jason was beginning to feel tired as he ran. It was like the entire school had been deserted and he was left with only the three bullies. As he ran, he wished he possessed the power of Nero. This was the perfect time for him to show them that they were messing with the wrong person. He desperately wanted to create a fire blaze like Nero and scare them off. This would make sure they never bothered him again! He wished he was living in the world of those superheroes, where magic was possible. Unfortunately, there was nothing like that in this world. This reality did not allow such kinds of magic. The only way he could save himself was by making sure they never caught up with him.

"Stop running!" Anderson was calling. Jason could feel the anger in the pursuer's voice. He was getting increasingly infuriated at Jason for making them run so much.

Jason turned into another corridor again and tripped over a vacuum cleaner that had been left carelessly there. He fell on his face. Before he could rise up again to continue running, the boys caught up with him. As he stood to his feet, he was grabbed by both arms by Greg and Anderson.

"Hello," Matt said menacingly, standing before him. "You really can run very fast."

"Let me go," Jason struggled with his captors, "Let me go right now!"

"And what are you going to do if we don't?" Matt asked.

"I'm going to scream."

The three exchanged glances and then burst into laughter.

"Oh you're going to scream," said Matt, "By all means, scream. Scream your lungs out. Nobody is going to come for your rescue."

He pinched Jasons' arm hard as he yelped! Greg and Anderson released Jason and he fell to the floor. Jason now had a nasty red mark on his arm.

"What do you have in the bag?" Greg asked. And without seeking permission, he reached out and pulled the bag off Jason's bag.

The three bullies ransacked the bag, looking for money or anything they could sell, or even gamble with in their playground dice games. Matt brought out Jasons trusty sketchpad and opened it.

"Oh, our dear Jason is an artist," he said mockingly, "He has drawn the picture of someone who will defend him. Oh, Mr Hero," he said to the image, "Come out and defend your boy. Come out now!"

All the three boys laughed. Jason wished Nero could actually come to his rescue right now. But it was impossible.

Chapter 3: A Window Of Opportunity!

Jason suddenly saw a window of opportunity as the three bullies continued glancing through the pictures he had drawn. He quickly rose to his feet and ran back in the direction he had come from. Before the three could react, he was already many steps ahead of them. This time around, he was running out of the school building into the compound. He could her them pursuing behind and calling on him yet again, but he was already far away from them. He crossed various corridors and eventually arrived at the exit of the building. As he stepped out of the building, he wanted to lock the door from outside, but there was no time to do that anymore. He looked around the compound and found the bicycles belonging to the bullies. Fortunately for him, one of the bicycles was unlocked. He rushed to it and picked it up, then he started pedaling away just as his pursuers came out of the building.

"He's riding my bike!" Matt yelled, "He's riding my bike!"

"Let's go after him!" Greg told Anderson.

The two ran to their bicycles and unlocked it.

"What about me?" Matt asked.

"You wait here. We'll catch him and get back your bike," said Greg.

"You can't leave me here!"

"Climb on my carrier" said Anderson, "Come on, be fast about it. He's getting away!"

Matt climbed behind Anderson and the three continued to chase Jason.

Jason pedaled the bicycle as fast as he could. He needed to be as far away from his pursuers as possible. He had missed the bus and his only hope of escaping was taking the bike. He knew taking other peoples property was wrong, but he was in desperate trouble! Jason rode the bike to the train station where he planned to take the next available train home. His arm was really stinging from the pinch he has received! Jason suddenly heard the sound of a bell. He looked behind him and saw the bullies. They were speeding towards him. Apparently, he had borrowed the slowest bicycle out of the three. Jason started pedaling faster. He was terrified! If they caught up with him again, they would do terrible things to him. The bullies were determined to make his night a disaster. He was sweating profusely as he pedaled away. All he needed to do now was get to the train station before they caught up with him. The station would be crowded and the bullies would not be able to hurt Jason in the presence of other people. He might even disappear among the people at the train station. They would not find him.

He swore within himself that he would request for a change of school after today. He would not go back to that school, even if it meant going to a different school then Emily! He would explain to his parents what had been going on. He didn't care anymore if he would be called a telltale by his classmates. He would not be coming to the school anymore anyway. He wanted to further his education in another school. The bullies were making his life miserable, and it was only a matter of time for him to lose his rationality. The best solution was the change of school. He wished he could stand and defend himself, but that would be crazy! Jason knew he had to continue running and get to safety. He was still about ten minutes away from the train station. Jason became worries that he might not be able to make it. From all indication, it was obvious that the boys would catch him before he arrived at his destination. There was only one thing for him to do at this juncture – he must find a fortress. A sanctuary that would protect him from the clutches of these determined villains.

To the surprise of his pursuers, he pedaled off the road and entered a street. The three bullies had known his intention of going to the train station, but his sudden redirection took them all by surprise. They paused at the junction of the street, watching him as he pedaled down. Jason looked back and saw them at the junction. They were no longer following. At first he thought they were tired of pursuing him, but he was wrong. The pursuers turned their bicycles around and went west. They didn't follow down the same street as him. He wondered why that could be? Jason breathed a sigh of relief! Finally, he was rid of the troublemaking bullies. He slowed down his pace to catch his tired breath. He was now pedaling with calmness.

He stopped immediately when he suddenly saw an old video game store. Jason was enthralled by what he was seeing. Through the glass, he was able to see various types of games. He was excited! He had lived his whole life for games. He dismounted from the bicycle and leaned it against the window.

He walked into the store. He was struck with an open-mouthed excitement. There were various video games ranging from old to new. He walked through the shop. It was a retro video game store and there were thousands of video games covering the old, dusty, spiderweb covered walls! Jason wanted to have all the games so that he could spend the rest of his life playing them! There were video games in shelves, in glasses, on the walls and inside big cartons. The strangest thing that Jason noticed was that the store was deserted. It looked like a place that had been closed for many, many years. He wondered where the owner of the store was. What was the man doing by abandoning this fortress of paradise? Jason wanted to continue living in this store. He wanted to grow old while trying to complete every single one of the video games. He walked around the store, checking each game carefully and reading their back covers. For the first time in a long time, fate was smiling on him. He had the intention of taking home as many video games as possible. A part of his mind told him what he wanted to do was wrong, but it was not stealing if nobody came to claim it. It showed that this place had been abandoned for long.

Then something caught his attention. A video game controller. But, not just any video game controller. Jason had never seen anything like it! The controller was encased in a diamond box. Within the box was a dancing bolt of lightning! It was as if the controller was being protected by live electricity! On the case of the controller was a sign that read: 'DON'T TOUCH!'

Jason immediately stood back. Although he was mesmerized by the controller, he also felt like it was something dangerous. He was not eager to disobey the instruction on the sign.

Suddenly, there was a huge BAAAM! The door of the store was thrown open and the three bullies stepped in.

"This is the perfect spot for us to get you" Matt seethed, "How dare you take my bike?"

Jason was scared again. He had made the mistake of leaving the bike in front of the store. The bullies had found the bike and figured he was in the store. How could he be so careless? He had thought they had stopped pursuing him. It turned out that they had taken a different route to get here.

"What do you want from me?" Jason asked in a frustrated tone. He was tired of everything

"You think you're smarter than us, don't you?" said Greg, "Well, you're not. And we're going to make you pay for stealing our friend's bike." Greg punched his left hand into his right repeatedly and moved menacingly toward Jason.

Jason started to take steps backward.

"Where do you think you're going?" Anderson asked, "There's nowhere for you to hide this time around." He turned to his friends, "Boys, let's finish him now."

Jason immediately turned around and attempted to run but he tripped again and fell to the floor, mistakenly knocking the controller off the shelf! Jason banged his head against a hard game display and was knocked unconscious! The controller crashed to the floor and the thunder inside of it was let loose! There was a crack of thunder all around the shop! Consoles fell off shelves and fire sparkled from the ceiling.

The three bullies were scared. They did not understand what was going on. They saw Jason's unconscious body on the floor and assumed that they were in big trouble! They started screaming for help as the lightning continued raging all around the store. Eventually, they found their way out of the store and picked up their bikes. They pedaled to safety, far, far away from the shop. They had immediately forgotten about Jason, they didn't care if he was okay as long as they were safe. Then they had nothing to worry about. Besides, nobody saw them chasing Jason. There was no way him getting hurt would be linked to them. He had been hurt by the lightning that had come out of that controller right!? They saw it all. They would have been hurt too had they not escaped in time.

"No one can hear about this!" Greg barked at his friends.

"Of course," said Matt.

"Jason got what he deserved," added Anderson.

***

Back in the retro game store, Jason woke up after an hour of losing consciousness. As he slowly gained consciousness, he was immediately overwhelmed by a splitting headache. For a while, he didn't know where he was, or what had brought him there. All he knew was that he had woken up in a strange place filled with old Video games.

He rose to a sitting position and held his head in his left hand. He felt something heavy in his right hand and looked at it. He was holding a game controller in his right hand! Then, he remembered everything that happened. He had been chased by the three bullies and he had arrived here at the old store. They had found him here and tried to attack him when he tripped and fell. That was everything he remembered. He searched around, expecting to see the bullies lurking somewhere, waiting for him to wake up. But there was no sign of life in the store. He rose to his feet. The headache was beginning to subside. He walked out of the store. The bikes were no longer there. This meant one thing – his pursuers had left. He wondered what had made them leave. It was unlike them to leave just like that. Something MUST have happened. However, whatever happened, he was grateful that the three did not inflict any permanent damage on him and he was finally safe. He stared at the object in his hand. It was the same controller that had caught his interest when he was alone in the store. He inspected it carefully. The little bolt of lightning was still dancing in it! He could see it because even the controller itself was made of see-through glass. Perhaps this was what had chased his bullies off? Jason returned the old and mysterious controller to the shelf where he had seen it before, after deciding that he had no use for it. Initially, he had wanted to own everything in the store, but the recent events had made him grow tired of any further adventure for now.

Jason walked out of the store when he felt a warm glow behind him. A bright, glowing light was shimmering all around the old building! He looked to the ceiling, but the source of the light was not coming from there. He looked beside him and saw that the light was shining out from the controller! He walked slowly towards it. The heat from the bright glow was drawing him close as his disbelief and curiosity skyrocketed.

He gently picked it up and admired it again.

"Maybe it's talking to me?" Jason pondered to himself. "Maybe it wants me to take it home?"

He held the glowing controller firmly in his hand and walked out of the store. He eventually found his way back to his home. He knew exactly what he was going to do as soon as he arrived back in his bedroom. He would plug the old, mysterious controller into his video games console and see what would happen! Perhaps this controller would make Power Wolf Heroes more interesting to play.

He could not wait to see what the outcome would be!

Chapter 4: The old, Mysterious Controller

When Jason got home that day, he was too tired to do anything. He ached all over. Apart from the injury he got from falling in the games store, he had also been injured by the arm pinching he got from the bullies in school. He had decided that he would not be going back to that school tomorrow. He was tired of being constantly picked on by those boys. Even though he had promised his mother that he would not skip school again, this time around he would have to break his promise. His wellbeing was at stake here.

He would call his parents as soon as he cleaned up and got the red mark on his arm and the bump on his head treated. He would explain the circumstances surrounding his decision to no longer return to that school. The only regret he would have would be not seeing Emily again. He wished he had told Emily what was on his mind in the bus this morning, but Brian never gave him the chance. Brian had been there to ruin his plans. In a way, Brian was also a bully. The only difference between Brian and the other three was that Brian did not inflict any bodily pain on him; the kind of pain Brian inflicted was an emotional one.

Later in the evening the same day, Jason decided to play more video games before calling his parents. The game would help him relax his nerves and allow him think a lot more clearly. As he switched on the TV, his attention caught the old, mysterious controller that was sitting on his bedroom floor. He picked it up and plugged it into the video game console.

As soon as he plugged the controller, there was a flash of lightning! The entire room was lit up by bright lights coming from both the television and the controller. The lightning was like a bolt of electricity! Jason was scared. He did not understand what was going on. The light became brighter and brighter until he could take it no more. It was stinging his eyes so badly that he had to cover his face with his hands. Then in less than a minute, the bright light disappeared and everything became normal once again.

Jason took his hands off of his face and stared at the television. It had turned off completely. Even the games console and the controller had turned off too. Jason was confused. *"What's going on here?"* he wondered.

Jason suddenly felt that he was not alone in his room. There was an alert, tense feeling crawling up his spine. He was sure he had locked the door of his room; there was no way anyone in his family would enter if he didn't open the door. But regardless, he still felt that he wasn't alone. His suspicion was confirmed when he saw a shadow quickly dart across the wall! He turned around and screamed in fright at what he saw. He immediately stopped screaming when he saw the figure… He could not believe what he was seeing… Only one word escaped from his mouth…

"Nero!?"…

"*Saikzzo rhyyy wzasfkeeria ma?*" the figure proclaimed.

"I don't understand what you mean Nero! How did you get here!?"

The figure stopped and shut its eyes for a brief moment. Then its eyes opened and it said, "Who are you, my friend?"

"My name is Jason. How did you get here from the game world?"

"The game world?" asked Nero.

Jason continued, "Yes. You were a game character. I play as you as a character in my video game… Through my television… How come you are in my world, Nero?"

"I don't understand what is happening. You are Jason? You are the same person always speaking to me whenever I'm about to fight my enemies?" stuttered Nero.

"You always heard me?" Jason was utterly shocked.

Nero was somewhat amused at Jason's growing energy. "Yes. You always tell me what to do whenever I fight. It seems like you control my movement. I have always wanted to meet you, Jason."

"This is unbelievable!" Jason smiled. "It's nice meeting you too, Nero!"

He extended a hand for a shake and Nero stared at it in confusion.

"What is this?" the fighter asked.

"I'm offering you a handshake. Grab my hand."

As Nero grabbed his hand, Jason was thrown back to the bed by an electric shock!

"Why did you shock me?" He screamed.

"Shock you? How did I shock you?"

"You just shocked me with your hand! Why did you do that?"

"You felt a reaction when I grabbed your hand?"

"Yes!"

"That's so unfortunate. I hope you use it well."

"Use what well?" asked Jason.

"You will understand later," replied Nero.

"Do you know what brought you to my world?" asked Jason.

"No, I don't Jason."

"I think it's that controller that brought you back!" Jason continued.

"There's a bolt in it," Nero noticed.

"Yes, I don't know what that is," said Jason.

"And it's broken."

"I can see that too. How do I fix it?" Jason asked.

"I have no idea," replied Nero.

Jason thought of a solution. "Maybe I should take it to school tomorrow and show my Science teacher. He might be able to fix it."

"That's a good idea," replied Nero.

Jason cast his eyes downward. "Unfortunately, I have decided not to go to school anymore. There's no point going there."

"Why is that?" asked Nero.

Jason continued looking at the floor with a sad gaze. "I was beaten up by three boys today in school."

"Why?" Nero's curiosity was sparked.

"There is no reason. They are bullies. They just like hurting helpless people," continued Jason.

"Did they cause the mark on your arm?" Nero pointed down to Jasons red mark on his arm, which was now bruising.

"Yes," replied Jason glumly.

Nero moved closer to Jason and pointed to his arm. Suddenly, Jason felt pain leaving his injury where the bully pinched him. When Nero brought a finger to the spot of the injury, sparkles of energy power shined and healed the entire area!

"You have healed me, Nero!" shouted Jason excitedly.

"I gave you some of my life battery. I can heal some minor wounds, but I am powerless against major wounds," taught Nero.

"That's so cool!" Jason exclaimed, throwing his hands up in the air with a grin crossing his face.

Nero looked glum for a moment. "I need to get back to my world."

"How do we do that?" Jason asked.

"I don't know, but I need to get back. I can't stay in this world forever. This world is not meant for me. I must go back to my world and be a hero!" proclaimed Nero whilst placing his hands on his hips, pushing his chest out and gazing off into the distance heroically as if he were about to save the day.

"Can I follow you to your world? I think I prefer your world better then mine," asked Jason, with a gleam of hope in his eyes.

"What is wrong with your world?" asked Nero, tilting his head slightly with confusion and intrigue.

Jason began to tell Nero of his problems at school. "There are three boys making my life miserable in school. I have decided not to go back to that particular school because I am powerless against them. I will call my parents and inform them about my decision. I want to come to your world where I would be able to defend myself. I want to have superpowers too so that I can protect myself against enemies!"

"Don't make that decision yet," said Nero.

Jason frowned in confusion. "Why shouldn't I?"

Nero continued. "I want you to go to school tomorrow. If you still want to leave school after tomorrow, then I won't stop you. But you must understand that it's not possible for you to come to my world. It simply can't be done."

"Nothing is impossible, Nero," said Jason. "Look at you. If you can appear in my world, then I strongly believe that I can appear in your world too."

"I don't belong in this world. I need to return as soon as possible. How would you explain my presence here to other people?"

"I'll tell them you came from the video game world," begged Jason, dropping his arms to the ground, slumping his shoulders and lowering his gaze.

"What makes you think they will believe you?" asked Nero.

Jasons gaze lifted slightly to make eye contact with Nero. "Then I'll just tell them you're my friend," he mumbled quietly, with an essence of sadness in his voice.

Nero silently stared at Jason.

"I'm hungry, Nero. Will you join me for dinner?"

"I don't get hungry," stated Nero.

Jasons curiosity was sparked even further. "How do you survive if you don't eat?"

"In this world, oxygen is my food. I don't need anything else. As long as I'm breathing fine, then I'm good." Nero educated Jason calmly while casually looking around the bedroom, taking in all the details.

"That's so weird," Jason said, scratching his head.

"Go ahead and eat your food. When you return, we'll talk more. There must be a way for me to return to my world," pondered Nero.

That night, both Jason and Nero discussed at length about the video game world.

"Do you know Crackle?" Jason asked.

"Crackle is my good friend. He's a very good fighter!"

"Yes! I like how he fights. I wish I could fight like him!" shouted Jason with enthusiasm.

"I'm sorry, I can't teach you his fighting style. Only Crackle himself can teach you that," responded Nero while still calmly taking in the details of the bedroom.

"Maybe if I plug the controller into the game, Crackle would appear just like you appeared," said Jason with his eyes full of hope once again.

Nero shrugged. "Maybe."

"What about Ransin? Do you know Ransin?"

"Ransin is a thief," said Nero, folding his arms and frowning.

Jason was perplexed. "How?" he scoffed.

"She cheats when she fights. Don't be like Ransin. She's not a good role model for you."

"What makes you think she cheats?" asked Jason.

"She reads people's minds," Nero continued, his attention shifting from the bedroom surroundings to Jason.

Jasons confusion grew. "How is that cheating?"

Nero continued. "You are not supposed to intrude into people minds without their permission. Because she can read minds, she manipulates the decisions of her opponents. Whatever move you make is because she wants you to make it. That's not fair. It's not fair at all."

"But I think her superpower is cool," Jason whined.

Nero explained. "You only think it's cool because you're not her victim. Whatever you do, do not bring Ransin into this world. She will destroy things. She will make people go loopy! The minds of you humans are so fragile. She will have a field day controlling everyone. She might even start a war of the world. It's dangerous to bring Ransin into this world."

Jason understood. "Well, I'm not planning to bring everyone from Power Wolf Heroes into this world. As a matter of fact, I don't think I need to bring anyone else. I'm okay with only you. You can teach me how I can protect myself."

"I don't have to teach you," said Nero.

Jason was confused again. "Why not?" he asked.

"You shall know soon enough." Nero's gaze returned to the bedroom surroundings.

"Can you produce fire on your palm as you always do in the game?" asked Jason, changing the subject excitedly.

"Yes, indeed I can," answered Nero. "Would you like me to show you?"

"Oh, please do!" Jason was practically bouncing with excitement.

Nero stood up and flicked his fingers in both hands. Immediately, fire ignited from both hands, he spread his hands and the fire burned on his palms.

"It's burning on your palm," Jason said, astonished.

"Yes, it is," said Nero, raising one eyebrow and feeling pretty cool about himself.

Jason became concerned. "It will burn your skin."

Nero continued with his eyebrow still raised and a slight smirk on his face. "No, it can't. Fire is my friend. I'm forged from a volcano. I am fire. Fire is me."

"Wow, that's so cool!" Jason was impressed, "Can you throw them as you always do in your fights?"

"Yes, I can. Would you like me to throw one?" Nero began preparing a little fireball in his palm by spinning his hand in tiny circles.

"What would happen if you do?" asked Jason.

Nero's smirk dropped. "Whatever is in the fires path will be burnt to a crisp."

"Then please don't throw the fire at me," exclaimed Jason.

Nero closed his palm and the fire died off.

Jason continued. "Do you have any other power apart from the fire?"

"I am extremely strong," replied Nero.

"How strong?" Jasons returning excitement quickly replaced his concern for the fire.

Nero took a second to return to his heroic pose, closing his eyes and raising his eyebrows high. "Extremely strong, at least compared to the strengths of the humans of this world."

"That's so cool!" Jason could barely contain his energy.

Nero stared at him for a moment, perplexed. "Why do you keep saying cool?"

"Because you're cool."

"No, I'm not."

"You're not?"

Nero's hero pose returned. "I'm not cool, Jason. I'm as hot as molten lava! Only wimps are cool. I am a brave and confident hero."

Jason replied. "Okay, you're really boiling," said Jason, rolling his eyes.

"I wish I was like you, Nero."

"You're perfect the way you are, Jason," replied Nero.

"If I was perfect I wouldn't be a victim of bullies. I would be able to defend myself against them. But I always ended up getting the rough treatment." Jason paused and then added, "I want you to follow me to school tomorrow."

"Why should I do that?" asked Nero.

"I want you to protect me against the people bullying me, Nero. If you were with me, those boys would not be able to touch me." Jason looked at Nero with puppy dog eyes.

"Would your school allow me to follow you around?" asked Nero, scratching his head.

"Well, you can wait somewhere. The bullies always attack me after school hours. You can be there to protect me from them at the time."

Nero thought for a second. "Listen to me, Jason. I would follow you to your school if you really needed me. But trust me, you don't need me tomorrow. Just go there and be a nice kid. Don't draw any unnecessary attention to yourself. You will be fine, trust me."

Jason didn't seem to be reassured but he could see that Nero was not ready to follow him. "Okay, I will go tomorrow. If I return home with another pinch on my arm then I will blame you for it!"

Chapter 5: A Superhero Comes To Life

Jason went to school the following morning with a feeling of apprehension. He was not sure why he had listened to Nero's advice, but he could not disobey the superhero come to life; Nero was his favorite superhero after all. Because he expected to bump into his bullies, Jason refused to take the school-bus this time around. Instead, he went with his personal bike. If anything went wrong, he would be able to do a fast getaway with his own bike. His bike was fast, there was no way those three would catch up with him if he was using it.

Because he used his bike, he showed up late to school that morning. Class had already begun by the time he had arrived! The first thing Jason did as soon as he got to school was search for his school bag. He had left it behind when he was escaping from the bullies the day before! He walked to the hallways where he had left it, but the bag was nowhere to be found. He knew exactly where to go next. He would have to go and demand for the return of his bag from the three bullies. Surely, the bag must be with them. But he was scared too approach them. There was no doubt in his mind that they would pinch his arm again. Jason was sure that they would continue the torment from the previous day. He couldn't satisfy these bullies with a simple pinch like that. They had not put Jason through enough treatment yet. As he was walking toward the bullies class, he bumped into one of them in the hallway. His heart skipped a beat as soon as he spotted Greg!

"Hey buster!" said Greg, apparently surprised. "How come you're still alive? We thought you were a goner in the video game store last night."

Jason took careful steps toward Greg, his eyes gazing at the floor so as to not provoke him. "I just want my schoolbag. I'm not here for any trouble. Just give me my bag and I'll leave." Jason's voice was shaky.

Once again, the hallway was deserted. Every time he was at the mercy of the bullies, there was usually no one to rescue him. No teacher. No student. Just the bullies and him, alone.

Greg smiled wickedly, "You want your schoolbag huh?" he said, "Well, if you kneel before me, I may consider giving it to you."

"You want to humiliate me before you can give me my bag?" Jason's voice shook even more.

"If you really want your bag, you have to kneel before me. You have to acknowledge me as your master," Greg taunted, still smiling.

Jason knew he had no choice; there was nothing he would say that would make Greg change his mind. He always knew Greg as someone with a real mean streak. He was often behind the most wicked things. Greg had been expelled from his former school for attempting to trap a student in the stinky janitors closet! He was never remorseful for any of his cruel acts.

Jason gently went on his knees before Greg. "Can I have my bag now?" he asked, turning red from embarrassment.

"Beg for it," Greg continued to taunt.

"May I please have my bag?" Jason began to become more and more frustrated.

"Say that I'm the greatest of all time!" Greg said, still smiling wickedly.

"*What!?*" Jason was horrified.

"If you really want your bag, you have to say that I'm the greatest of all time."

"I'm not going to do that." Jason pushed back.

"Then you don't need your bag. I can just as well burn the bag and all the books inside."

"You wouldn't dare!" Jason panicked at the thought of loosing his sketchbooks and having all of his hard work destroyed.

Greg shrugged. "I can and I'm gonna. You watch and see. The only thing that will stop me from doing that is if you say that I'm the greatest of all time". He reached into his pocket and brought out his cellphone.

"What are you doing?"

"I want to record you saying that I'm the greatest of all time," he laughed "Anderson and Matt would love this."

"You are so evil, Greg. Do you know that?"

"Are you going to say that I'm the greatest of all time or not?" He had already pressed the Record button on his cell phone video camera.

Jason knew he had no choice but to do what Greg asked. If he didn't do it, Greg would burn his bag and his books. He could deal with the annoyance of the video circulating all around the school, but he could not bear his bag and books getting burnt to ash; especially his sketches of his superheroes. He wished Nero was here to witness what he was going through right now. He slowly lifted his head and brought his gaze to meet Gregs. Jason was just about to say what Greg wanted until suddenly Greg shouted "Take this, buster!"

Everything suddenly went into slow motion for Jason. He saw Greg's leg move backward and before he could kick him, Jason grabbed the leg in one hand. He couldn't believe his own strength! He looked up at Greg who was staring down at him in shock.

"What are you trying to do?" Jason asked.

"What do you think you're doing? Drop my leg right now!" Greg panicked, becoming more and more frustrated.

Still holding the leg in one hand, Jason stood to his feet. Greg was bouncing like a duck on water as Jason held the leg firmly.

"Drop my leg right now!"

Jason dropped the leg. "Now where is my bag?"

"How dare you hold my leg?" barked Greg. He clenched his hand into a pinching grasp and attempted to strike Jason. Again, his action was in slow motion to Jason, who grabbed the hand before it struck him. Jason couldn't believe what was going on! He was confused. Things were happening beyond his comprehension. Did he all of a sudden posses superhuman powers?

With his other hand, Jason decided to flick Gregs forehead lightly to gesture him to back off. To his utter shock, the impact of the flick threw Greg across the hallway! He watched in horror as Greg flew in the air and landed six feet away from him.

"You're crazy!" Greg screamed, "You're totally crazy!" He was trying to rise to his feet. Jason quickly ran to him. In a split second, he was in front of Greg again. He was not only strong, he was also fast.

"Give me your cellphone," he told Greg.

This was the first time he had seen a bully worried! Jason never thought he would see this day. He was highly proud of himself. Now he understood why Nero had persuaded him to attend school today. Nero had given him some of his powers when they shook hands. That was why he was jolted by a bolt of electricity back in his bedroom!

Greg immediately handed over his phone to Jason.

"Thank you, Greg. You will get back your cell phone when you return my bag. I'll be waiting for you." Said Jason heroically, releasing Greg from his grasp.

"You're crazy!" Greg said as he limped away quickly.

Jason stood in the hallway with his jaw dropped in astonishment. He looked down at his hands. "Could I be a super hero too?"

***

Greg still could not believe what had just happened to him. He had just been whooped by a scrawny twelve-year-old. He was ashamed of himself. Something was not right about Jason. Within the hours of yesterday and today, the boy had become very powerful. Nobody had ever thrown him with a flick as much as he was thrown by Jason. It was like the boy had been possessed by a kind of supernatural power. He could not even explain how something like that could be possible. He needed to tell Matt and Anderson about what had just happened. He waited till the end of the class before calling on his friends.

"You look agitated," said Matt, "what's wrong?"

"It's Jason," Greg replied immediately.

"Jason? Who is Jason?"

"The one who stole your bike yesterday."

"Oh, that boy? What's up with him? I thought he was a goner in the old video games store yesterday," replied the bully.

"Apparently not. Something strange has happened to him. he's no longer the boy we used to pick on."

"What are you talking about?" asked Anderson.

"Jason has become very strong!"

"I still don't understand what you're saying, Greg. Are you sure you're okay? Why are you sweating like this?"

"I was whooped by Jason," said Greg, staring at the floor shamefully.

Matt and Anderson exchanged a glance, then they suddenly burst into laughter.

"You should be a comedian," said Matt laughing hard at what he just heard. "You'll make a great career from making people laugh."

But Greg was not smiling with them. "I'm serious here. Jason is back with a vengeance and he wants his bag back."

The laughter disappeared from the two friends' faces. "He's really back? He's really not a goner?"

"What makes you think I'll be joking about something like that?" Replied Greg.

"So the boy lives." A frown appeared across Andersons face.

"And he's also powerful," Greg said with a shaky voice.

"Where is he now?" asked Anderson, "I won't believe you until I meet him again in person".

"I don't know, but I think we need to wait for him after the end of school today," answered Greg.

"This time around, we won't let him slip away," added Matt.

"I think we need to carry his bag along. That may be the only thing that can save us from him. The boy has become crazy, I tell you. He's no longer the scared little kitten he was yesterday."

***

For the rest of the school hours, Jason did not see any of the bullies. It was as if they were avoiding him. He waited in places he knew they always hung out, but none of them revealed themselves. Perhaps Greg had informed them about his superpowers and they were scared of bumping into him.

But unknown to Jason, the three bullies had been stalking him since his little dramatic episode with Greg. They had kept themselves hidden as they followed him everywhere. They had been waiting for the right moment to strike.

Eventually, Jason gave up the thought of seeing the three bullies again. Now he believed that they were indeed scared of him. They were keeping as far away from him as they could. He returned to his bike and climbed it. He pedaled away; he could not wait to meet Nero and explain how he dealt with Greg. He was sure that Nero would be very proud of him. He had been given the power so that he could protect himself, and that was exactly what he had done. Nero would be impressed when he heard the news.

He looked behind him and saw the three bullies following behind on their own bikes! The last time he had been so scared that he pedaled away with all his strength. This time around, Jason did not even bother increasing his pace. He continued his journey without worrying himself about the three people coming to pick on him. He felt very strong; there was nothing any one of them could do that would be capable of hurting him.

A short while later, the three boys caught up with Jason. Matt overtook him with a bicycle. Jason was forced to stop. He didn't like stopping in-between journeys. Although he had stopped the bicycle, he didn't entirely get off it. He rested his arms on the handle and stared at the three boys before him.

"Hello, which one of you nice young men has brought me my bag?" Jason asked them.

The boys looked at one another. They had been waiting for something to come out of Jason's mouth, and this was definitely not what they thought he would say. The boy's confidence had suddenly skyrocketed. Maybe Greg had been right when he told them about Jason this morning.

The three boys got down from their bikes and slowly approached Jason.

"How can I help you boys?" Jason asked them.

"I can see that you've truly grown a spine. Well, I'm going to get you. Nobody goes against any one of us," threatened Anderson.

While all this was going on, Greg had started taking some wise steps backwards. Matt was getting off his bicycle.

"Where is my bag?" said Jason firmly.

"By the time we finish with you, you will wish you had never gone against us. We will not only pinch you, but we're also going to take your bike!" said Matt.

Jason smiled and replied them calmly. "Bring it on."

Chapter 6: These couldn't be real super powers?

"Both of you get him!" Anderson told Greg and Matt.

"I'd rather stay here," Greg replied, still backing away.

"Darn it, Greg!" said Matt. He walked close to Jason and attempted to grab him. Jason quickly grabbed his hand and shot a fire beam around his wrist that warped into a magical hand cuff! Matt screamed out "Let go of my wrist! Let go!"

"When you stop being mean," said Jason.

"Please, please. Release me, please." Matt already had panic in his eyes.

Jason threw off the magic handcuff and flicked Matt. Like Greg, Matt flew in the air and landed six feet away! Anderson watched what was happening with his eyes filled with disbelief. What he was seeing was humanly impossible, yet it was happening. A twelve-year-old boy had just thrown Matt away as if his friend was a basketball. Where had Jason received these powers?

"I just want my bag and I'll be on my way" Jason said calmly, "I don't want any trouble."

"You whooped my friends because of your bag?" asked Anderson.

"I only want what belongs to me," replied the hero, "You all have picked on me for a lot less. But I'm not a bully like any one of you. I just want my bag and to go home. I don't want any problems."

"You can't say that after throwing Matt away like a soda can. I'm going to make you pay."

Anderson started running toward Jason. His hand was clenched in a punch and it was raised, ready to strike Jason. He was moving very fast, but to Jason, his movement was in slow motion. Anderson neared Jason. But before he could land the first punch, Jason shot a protective magical wall of fire in front of his own feet to stop Andersons attack. Anderson stopped in his tracks; he was momentarily disoriented. For a while, he was totally confused about his surroundings. He couldn't believe what he was seeing! These couldn't be real super powers? He took three steps backward and landed on his backside. Then he began to cry like a baby.

Jason walked past him and toward Greg who was holding the schoolbag. "Please give me my bag now."

Greg immediately handed the bag over to the owner. "Take your bag. I don't want any trouble please."

Jason collected the bag and returned to his bike. Before pedaling away, he turned to the three boys and said. "I hope you boys have learnt your lesson. It is wrong to bully helpless people. I sincerely hope you have turned a new leaf. The world can be hard enough. You don't have to make it miserable for the people in it. Live and let live."

He pedaled away.

The three boys watched him as he moved. None of them were badly hurt, but they had been shaken with fear and amazement all at once! They had just been whooped by a little boy who did not even break a sweat while doing it.

"How did he become so suddenly powerful?" Greg asked. He was still in shock by what Jason had done.

Matt picked himself up from the dirt he had been thrown into. He was dusting off his body as he said, "I think it has something to do with what happened in that old video game store."

Anderson nodded his head. "I agree with you. Something strange happened in that store yesterday. I think he got his power from that place. I suggest we go to that store and find out what really happened."

The three boys agreed to visit the mysterious retro video game store once again. They picked themselves up and returned to their bikes. In twenty minutes they were back to the store.

"I don't think it's safe for us to go in," said Greg. "Do you remember what happened the last time? We were almost struck by a bolt of lightning."

"I think it's that same lightning that gave him his power," answered Matt. "Come on, we just have to check out what happened. We need to find out."

The three boys walked into the store. The whole building was dark. They could barely see in front of them. "Can someone find the light switch? Let's turn on the lights here. I can't see a thing," said Greg.

Matt searched around the walls and eventually came across a switch. He flicked it on and every lightbulbs in the store came on in a flash! The store was brightly illuminated and the boys could see every cobweb and old dusty video game. The boys moved around, searching for nothing in particular. They had come here for whatever could explain Jason's superpowers. The store was a lot bigger than they had initially thought. It was like an abandoned warehouse. There were thousands of various games arranged neatly in their boxes and placed on shelves, gathering dust.

"Jason likes playing games," said Matt.

"He does?" asked Anderson. "How did you know that?"

"You remember Shane from school? He once visited Jason at his house. He said the boy spends the whole day playing some kind of boring game with old graphics."

"Does that mean that he took a game from this store when he woke up?"

"That's what we're here to find out."

They walked to the spot where Jason had fainted when they tried to attack him that night. "This is the spot where he fell and lost consciousness," said Anderson, "Look at that broken glass."

"That's not glass," said Matt, "That's diamond!"

The two boys stared at him as if he had gone mad. "Diamond?"

"Yes. I have seen it before somewhere. That's definitely diamond."

"Does this mean we'll be rich if we gather up the diamond?"

Matt shrugged. "I guess so. If we can find someone to sell the diamond to, yes, we'll be rich."

"That's not why we're here, boys" said Greg, "Don't forget the mission." He suddenly stopped.

"What's wrong, Greg?"

"The controller is gone."

They frowned. "What controller are you talking about?"

"I remember, there was controller encased in a glass box sitting in this shelf. I think the shattered diamond is the glass case I'm talking about. When Jason fell, he knocked over the case. I think that's what brought about the lightning strike."

"So Jason took this controller?" asked Anderson "Why would he do that? Of all the games in the shop, he took just a controller?"

"That's what it seems like," answered Greg, "I think it's that controller that gave him his power."

"Why don't we find another controller?" asked Matt, "We can get our power from one too."

"I don't think there's any other controller like that. I noticed that particular one because of the sign placed on it – DON'T TOUCH. And also because it glowed. It was the source of light when we came into the store. It's a special kind of controller."

Anderson suddenly smiled. "Are you guys thinking what I'm thinking?"

"What are you thinking?"

"There's only one solution for us. We'll steal that controller from Jason."

"How would we do that?" asked Matt.

"We'll sneak into his house and take it. We only have to touch it and we'll become as powerful as Jason, if not more. When we take the controller and claim it, it's only a matter of time before the power departs from him. Then we'll punish him for what he did to us."

"That's so brilliant!" said Matt.

"How do we get to Jason's house?" asked Greg, "I don't know where he lives."

"I do," answered Matt, "I also know that he's the only one at home most of the time. His parents are always out on a trip. An old nanny always takes care of him in his parents' absence. Don't worry about her, she's not a threat to us."

"Good," said Anderson, "we don't have all day. Let's get to his house now."

"Wait," said Greg. "I think we need to do this in a smarter way. How do we get the controller without Greg knowing? You know the three of us cannot match him in strength. How do we get the controller without getting beaten up again by him?"

"It's simple. You and I will call him out to the front yard and get his attention directed on us. Then Matt would go into the house through the back door. He would sneak into his room and pick up the controller. Easy peasy."

"No, I'm not risking my wellbeing again. Your plan is a very dangerous one. I refuse to be used as the bait here," Matt said, shaking his head in disagreement.

"Come on, Matt. It's perfectly safe for you. If anyone would be the bait then that would be me and Greg. You're not putting yourself in danger. All you have to do is pick up the darn controller."

"Have you forgotten what happened the last time the controller was messed with? There was lightning. No, I don't want to touch that thing. I would be the one electrocuted to smithereens, not you."

Anderson sighed in frustration. He turned to Greg, "Would you like to go in place of the wimp?"

"I'm not a wimp!" protested Matt.

"Well, you look like one to me. You're a stinky chicken," teased Anderson.

"I think I have a better idea," said Greg calmly, "Why don't we wait till tomorrow."

"Tomorrow? Why should we wait that long?"

"All we have to do is skip school for a day. We'll go to his house when Jason goes to school tomorrow. Before he returns, we'll pick up the controller and disappear. The next time he sees us, we'll already have become a lot more powerful. Then we can conveniently get him!"

"Wow! That's a perfect plan," said Anderson, "We'll sneak into his room when he's in school tomorrow. It's perfect, just perfect."

"Now let's plan for tomorrow."

***

Jason arrived home feeling elated. Everything he wished had come to pass. He had wished that Nero could be in this world with him and it had happened. He had also wished that he had superpowers. That too had also been manifested into his life. It seemed like there was great power in his wishes. As soon as Jason got home, he went straight to his room, hoping to find Nero. But the room was devoid of anyone. He dropped his bag and searched around. There was no trace of Nero in the room.

"Nero, where are you?"

Jason went on all fours and searched under the bed. Still, there was no Nero anywhere. He began to think that maybe the superhero had found a way to return to his game world.

"Why would you leave without telling me," Jason was disappointed. "I thought you were my friend."

"I'm still your friend, Jason," he heard a familiar voice behind him. He turned around swiftly and saw Nero standing in his battle regalia.

"I've not left yet."

"Then where did you go?"

"I didn't go anywhere. I was in this room."

"But you were nowhere to be found when I entered this room."

"Yes, I was in an invisible mode."

Jason opened his mouth wide in surprise. "You can disappear?"

"Yes, basically. I can make myself invisible if I want to. It's one of the perks of being a superhero. You discover new powers about yourself every day."

"You've got some very impressive gifts, Nero."

"How was school today?"

Jason broke into a broad smile. "You gave me your powers, Nero. Is that why you convinced me to go back to school?"

"Indeed yes, I persuaded you to return to school."

"That's because you knew that I would be able to take care of myself."

"I didn't want to give up your dream of becoming a video game designer. How do you become that if you don't attend classes?"

Jason was utterly amazed. "How in the world did you know that I wanted to become a game designer?"

"You reveal a lot of your secrets whenever you play your game. Even though I concentrated on my fighting, I still heard everything you always said when you played. You have a girl you like; her name is Emily. There's a teacher you don't like. His name is Mr Stintson. And you're allergic to cats."

"You're really creepy, do you know that?" Jason smirked.

"I'm only telling you everything you say when you play your game," responded Nero.

Jason's eyes suddenly brightened up. "I have an idea!"

"I hope it's a good one."

"Yes, it is very good. Since you can make yourself invisible you can be my chaperone to school, Nero."

"Why do you need me to chaperone you?"

"Knowing that you're with me, I won't feel lonely. Besides, the power you gave me has expired. I'll need you in my corner incase those boys come to attack me again."

"I don't think it's a good idea."

"It's very easy. All you have to do is remain invisible. Nobody will see you."

"Tell me the exact reason you want me to accompany you to school."

Jason sighed. "Okay, it's Emily."

"The girl you like?"

The boy nodded shyly.

"Why do you need me?"

"I want to talk to her today. I want you to guide me on what to say."

"I do not have any experience about that."

"Just tell me what you think I should say so that I don't embarrass myself."

"Okay."

"I can hear you when you talk in your invisible state, right?"

"I'll program myself to allow only you to hear me."

Jason's eyes brightened up. "You can do that?"

"Yes, of course. Only you will be able to see me and hear me. I'll be like your personal ghost."

Jason laughed. "You also have a sense of humor."

Chapter 7: "He Seems To Have Gone Crazy"

The following morning, the three boys were already watching Jason's house. They were waiting for him to leave before stepping into the house and taking the controller. After about fifteen minutes, they saw Jason walk out of his home. To their surprise, the boy did not take his bike, neither did he follow the school bus that had initially parked in front of the house.

"Why is he talking to himself?" Matt asked.

"He seems to have gone crazy," noted Anderson.

"Could it be the controller that turned him into this?" Matt asked, he was beginning to get worried.

"Possibly," answered Greg.

"Oh my goodness!" said Matt. "I'm not touching that controller. I don't want to go insane like Jason."

"What nonsense are you talking about? No one will go insane."

"Jason is having a conversation with himself! If that's not crazy enough, I don't know what is."

"Get off your stupidity wagon and let's go," said Anderson. "It's time for us to go in the house. The boy has gone out of sight."

They came out of their hiding and entered the house through the back door. They located Jason's room and stepped inside.

"Wow!" said Matt, "His room is like a palace. See a lot of toys!"

"That's not what we're here for, Matt. Let's search around for the controller. We have to be very fast."

They began to search around the room.

"It's somewhere around. I can feel it" said Greg.

After about five minutes of searching, Matt spoke, "Here it is."

They all followed his direction and found the controller lying on a shelf that contained books. If not for Matt's sharp eyes, they wouldn't have seen it. It was lying inconspicuously between two books.

"It's broken," said Greg.

"Maybe it broke in the store when the lightning struck," said Matt.

"Let's pick it up and leave," Anderson said impatiently.

"And who is going to pick it up?" asked Matt, "It's definitely not going to be me. It still has the lightning burning in it. I'm not going to risk get shocked over that thing."

"I'm not touching it either" said Greg, "That thing is broken. It's dangerous to touch it."

Anderson stared at his friends frustratedly. "You're both big wimps!"

He brought out a handkerchief from his pocket and with it he cautiously picked up the controller. The boys breathed a sigh of relief. "Now let's leave."

They all scurried out of the house with Anderson in the lead.

***

"You just have to keep calm," Jason told Nero, "Nobody is going to know anything if you remain calm."

"I think you should talk less. People are starting to look at you like you have gone nuts."

"Oh!"

"Nobody, except you, can see or hear me. When you speak to me, they will assume you're talking to yourself. Only talk to me when there's no one watching you."

"Okay."

And so they continued the journey to school in silence. When they were alone for a brief moment, Jason said, "That's Emily going to class."

"Good," said Nero, "all you need is confidence. Every one likes confidence. If she notices that you lack confidence, she will never take you seriously. That's probably why you think she does not want to be your friend."

Jason turned to face Nero, he looked around to make sure that no one was staring at him. "I thought you said you knew nothing about this kind of stuff?"

"I know nothing," replied Nero.

"Then where did that one come from?"

"I read some online articles on your computer at home when you were in school yesterday. I did it just to keep myself busy."

"Wow! That's so cool!"

Nero stared at him.

"Oh, boiling, sorry. That's so boiling!" Jason corrected himself, "Now let's go to class."

They both entered the class. While Jason went to take his seat in the middle of the class, Nero stayed at the back, watching over the boy. Only Jason was able to notice his presence; his classmates had no idea that there was a stranger in class with them. The history teacher stepped into the class. He was a bespectacled middle-aged man who was fond of straightening his tie in every moment.

"Today, we're going to discuss the world war," began the man, "Who can tell me when the First World War began and ended?"

The class was silent. Apparently, no one among the students knew the answer to such a question.

"It started in 1914 and ended in 1918," said Nero.

Jason spoke up immediately "It started from 1914 to 1918."

"And that's correct!" said the teacher, highly impressed.

The other students in the class stared at Jason as if he were an alien. Emily in particular, looked at him with interest. Their eyes met and they smiled at each other. Nero noticed the potential friendship between the two and smiled too.

The teacher asked other tougher questions and Jason was giving the perfect answers, owing much to the assistance of Nero, whose robotic mind had downloaded the whole encyclopedia of the world. Everyone in class was amazed at his intelligence.

After the lecture Emily came to sit with him.

"How did you know all those tough answers?" she asked, obviously interested in his newfound knowledge.

Jason shrugged. "I have read them somewhere before, I guess."

"You seem like a very broad reader, Jason."

The boy had no response to give to that statement. He was becoming nervous. He realized that Emily had found him interesting and that was beginning to unnerve him. He had never gotten this kind of special attention from anyone, let alone Emily of all people.

"Calm down, Jason," Nero said close to him. "Do not scare her off with your weirdness. She's interested in being your friend. Try to make the conversation flow. Don't be a bore."

"Tell me, Emily, what are your interests?" asked Jason

She seemed to like the question. "I want to be an acrobat. I have been practicing after school."

"That's so cool."

"Ask her about her friends." said Nero

"Tell me about your friends." Asked Jason.

"My friends?" she seemed surprised by the question.

"Yes, your friends. How many friends do you have?"

"Well, I'm not one to keep friends. I have only two friends; one in school and the other in my neighborhood. You know my school friend don't you?"

Jason nodded.

Emily continued "It's just that I don't really keep friends that often. I like my close circle."

"Do you have any plan of having any more friends in future?" asked Jason.

She shrugged. "Maybe, how come?"

Jason turned to her. "I would like to be your friend, Emily, if you don't mind."

"Attaboy!" Nero said from the background.

Emily stared at Jason in surprise. "Wow! Something has changed about you," she smiled, "you have become different."

"How am I different? Asked Jason. I don't understand what you mean."

"Well, you have become more confident," she responded, "you're now bolder and suddenly more knowledgable. A lot of things have changed about you overnight."

Before Jason could respond, Brian appeared and said to Emily, "Hi Emily, may I see you for a moment? I have something more important to talk to you about than whatever it is that you are talking about with that loser" Brian gestured to Jason.

"I am talking to her right now, Brian. And that was a very rude thing to say. I'm sure Emily will speak to you once we are done with our conversation." Jason kept his cool but was firm with Brian.

"Get lost!." barked Brian.

"Brian, you are being rude and I am having a conversation with Emily. Please wait your turn," replied Jason calmly.

Brian was shocked by the response. He had never thought in a million years that Jason would have the confidence to talk to him in that manner. He watched as the boy continued his conversation with Emily.

Jason was surprised at his own level of confidence. The same Jason that had always been an object of bullying and mockery was now standing up for himself and being assertive.

Emily stared at him proudly. She loved the way he spoke to Brian. She had always seen Brian as kind of a misbehaved kid who liked making other people feel bad about themselves. It was so good seeing him perplexed by Jason's words.

Brian was white in the face with anger. He was short of the perfect response to give because he was baffled. He had no doubt that Jason had calmly one upped him. He could hardly believe what he was witnessing. He gathered himself and walked away.

Jason turned to Emily, "Why do you always allow Brian to talk to you as if he were your big brother?"

"Everybody in class is scared of him," she replied.

"Well, I'm not," announced Jason bravely.

"You used to be," responded Emily.

"I'm not scared of him anymore. And you shouldn't be either. He's such a bully. I don't like bullies. It's time for us to stand up against bullies. We must not always allow them to ruin our moods. It's not worth it."

"Wow! Jason, you have really changed."

"You haven't answered my question, Emily." Said Jason, changing the subject.

"And what question is that?"

"Would you like to be my friend?"

"Oh yes Jason, I would like to be your friend."

They smiled at each other.

Jason was in a very happy mood throughout that day. Nero had taught him how to defend himself against bullies. He had also taught him how to be the person he was meant to be. He had developed his confidence. Now people like Brian would not want to mess with him. If he could hold his head up high before Brian in the class then the others would learn to respect him.

"Thank you, Nero," Jason said as they walked out of the school gate, "You have helped me a lot."

"I only pushed you in the right direction. You did everything else yourself. The best thing a person can do is have confidence and believe in themselves. With confidence, there is nothing you cannot achieve in this life."

"You're right, Nero. I have become a new person because I am now confident. I don't think there's anything I can't achieve."

"The sky is your limit if you believe in yourself," said Nero, proudly.

Chapter 8: "You've Got To Fix The Controller"

The three boys took the controller to an open field where they would be able to escape if anything went wrong. Anderson still held it gingerly in his hand with the handkerchief; he was scared of the bolt of lightning dancing in it, but he didn't want his friends to notice his fear. When they got to the middle of the field, he placed the object on the ground.

"Who will go first?" he asked as he dropped the controller.

There was not a sound among them. After a long moment of silence, Greg decided that he would touch the object first. Every step he took towards it was responded by a step backward by his scared friends. Matt believed that one of two things would happen to Greg if he touched the controller. He would either go insane or be blown to smithereens. Matt didn't want to stick around when the latter happened. He stayed far away from the object and watched from afar.

Greg bent down and pointed out a finger toward the object on the ground. He was sweating profusely because he was scared of what might happen to him. When his hand touched the controller, he nearly fainted with fright. But there was no reaction. He did not feel anything. He tapped the object very fast again, still there was no reaction.

"Nothing is happening," he told his friends.

"I think you need to wait a few second before taking off your hand."

Greg attempted to touch the object again. This time, he waited five seconds before taking off his hand. Still, he felt nothing.

"Okay, let me try it," said Anderson.

He stepped forward and tapped the object, just like Greg had done the first time. He felt no reaction from the controller either. He touched it again, holding it for a few second this time.

"I feel nothing either."

"I think the controller is damaged," said Greg. "It's broken and I don't think there's a way we can fix it."

"Why doesn't Matt try holding it? It might work for him."

"No," said Matt, "I'll pass."

"Come on, Matt," urged Anderson, "it won't bite you."

"I don't want to fry."

"It doesn't hurt. Stop being a baby."

Matt reluctantly moved close to the object and touched it lightly. He felt no reaction.

"Okay, it's not working for me either," he said.

"Touch it again!" said Greg.

"But I already did."

"You only tapped it. You have to touch it for some seconds like the rest of us did."

Matt hated this. He hated it immensely. He was being forced to put his wellbeing in danger all because they wanted to get back at Jason. "Was all this worth it?" he wondered. He didn't sign up for this kind of risk at all. He moved over to the controller again and touched it. This time around, he surprised his friends. He grabbed it firmly in his hands, shutting his eyes tightly, expecting to be scattered by the bolt in it. But there was still no reaction. He opened his eyes and smiled.

"It's not working," he said. He lifted the object up from the ground. "It's not working at all. We have only been wasting our time."

"I'm sure this is what gave Jason his power. If we can find a way to fix it, then it will work for us." Greg said.

"How do you think we can fix it?" asked Anderson.

"I suggest that we continue tailing Jason."

"Why should we do that?"

"Did you notice that he was talking to himself?" I think it was this controller that makes him act like this. While he's talking to himself, he'll reveal how we can get it to work. He might say how he got it to work for himself."

"Okay. So we continue to watch him until he speaks about how to fix it?"

"Exactly."

"Why don't we give up already?" asked Matt. He was getting tired of the whole shenanigan. "Let's just leave the boy alone. We've taunted him enough, haven't we?"

"I can't believe you're saying this, Matt," said Greg, "Jason beat us all up."

"That only happened because we wanted to get him. If we had left him alone, we wouldn't have gotten beaten up."

"You're talking nonsense Matt," said Anderson "If you don't top saying this rubbish, we'll denounce you from the group."

"What group? A group that is mean to others? If you don't change your ways, then I don't want to associate myself with your bad ways. I'm not brought up to be a bully. I'm tired of proving what I'm not to either of you. You are taking things too far. You have made me act like a bad person. You made me risk my wellbeing because you're blinded by vengeance on someone who didn't even do anything wrong to begin with. I'm sorry, I can't be a part of this terrible group anymore."

"Then leave!" screamed Greg, "You think we can't do without you? We will be fine without you, you wimp. When we become powerful, we will punish both you and Jason. Go back to him. Kneel before him. Beg him to take you in as his sidekick, because you are nothing more than a wimpy sidekick. Go to away and stay there, Matt. We don't want someone like you here. Leave! Leave right now!"

"I'm highly disappointed in you, Matt," said Anderson, "we brought you in because we thought you had potential. We thought you had the power to be a leader. But you have just proved that you are not worthy of our group. You are free to leave. We are not going to miss you when you do."

"Very well then," said Matt, "I would like to disassociate myself from you both."

***

"I need to return to my world," said Nero. "My job is done here."

"How do we take you back?"

"You've got to fix the controller. That's the only thing that can take me back."

"How do I fix it? I don't know anything about it."

"What you need to do is very simple," said Nero. "A tiny cord has broken in the element, you've got to solder it back in its place. Afterwards, you plug it into your games console."

Jason frowned, "But that was the same thing I did that brought you back. What if I plug it into the game and it brings back another superhero?"

"There's gotta be something that must be done. I think we have no choice but to plug it in. If it brings in more heroes, we'll deal with it."

"All right. Let's go home. I have a soldering machine. You'll have to pull me through. You know I don't have my powers anymore."

"Okay."

They continued the journey.

***

Greg and Anderson were hiding in the bush listening to Jason.

"Who do you think he's talking to?" Anderson asked.

"I think he's delirious," replied Greg, "I don't care about that. What I care about is what he just said. He said he does not have his power anymore."

"And so?"

"Are you kidding me? This is the time for us to beat him up. Now that his power is gone we're perfectly safe."

"How about fixing the controller?"

"We don't have to worry about the controller for now. Let's first go and deal with the boy. Keep the controller here in the bush. He doesn't have to know that we have it. We'll fix it later. You heard what he said, right? He'll fix the controller with a soldering machine. I have a soldering machine at home. As soon as we beat him up, we'll take the controller to my house and fix it. Then it would give us the superpower we want."

Anderson smiled. "That sounds like a very good idea."

They left the controller in the bush and presented themselves before Jason.

"Here you are," said Greg, "now you're going to pay heavily for laying your hand on us."

Jason stared at them as if they were as boring as his homework and yawned.

"What do you want for me again?" he asked.

"We want to teach you a lesson you will never forget in your life."

"And how do you plan to do that?"

"By whooping you from here to Wisconsin," answered Greg.

Jason laughed. "It seems like you want to flicked six feet again. This time, i'll flick you even farther than the last time."

"You think we don't know that you don't have your powers anymore?"

"We heard you when you said your power was gone," said Anderson. Now we're going to make you pay severely for what you did. You dare lay your hands on us. Do you know who we are?"

"You're a bunch of bullies, that's who you are," answered Jason. "And you deserved every bit of punishment you received. You have always been picking on me since the day I joined your school. But that is not going to happen again. You will never bully me or anyone else again. I'll make sure of that."

The two boys laughed at how ridiculous Jason sounded to them. "What are you going to do? Get us again? You've lost your power, remember?"

Jason carried a smile on his face. "I'm not going to be the one to get you."

Greg and Anderson exchanged glances. They turned to Jason and asked, "Who is going to fight your battles for you? There's no one here to save you."

"Oh, but there is."

"Where's the person? We can get them too."

"He's standing behind you."

They quickly turned around but found nobody. They turned back to Jason. "Are you trying to be smart with us?"

"No, look behind you again."

They turned around and witnessed the tallest and strongest person they had ever seen. He was huge! Anderson recognized him immediately as one of the superheroes Jason had drawn in his sketch.

"This is impossible!" he whispered in shock.

"Oh my goodness!" exclaimed Greg "What a huge super hero!"

And before they could do anything, Nero grabbed them by their collars with each hand and lifted them off their feet. The two bullies struggled and clutched at his hands.

"Should I fling them away like rabbits?" teased Nero.

"No, don't hurt them. Just let them go."

Before placing them down, Nero snarled at the boys. "You stay away from Jason, right? If I see you being mean to him again then I will flick you both into space! Don't you ever dare me."

He placed them gently on the ground and released his hold on their collars. They coughed vigorously and ran away quickly. They looked like a pair of dogs that had just heard a firework. Jason laughed out loud as he watched the two bullies scurry away.

"Those are the boys bothering you?"

Jason nodded. "There is a third boy. I don't know why that one is not with them. The three are always together. I wonder where he is."

"Well, I don't think you should ever be scared of those two. They're bullies; you're a lot better off than them."

"But what if they return after you have gone back to your world? How do I protect myself from them? They might be even meaner this time around."

"Don't fret, my friend. There's no way those two are ever being mean to you again. I will always be with you, even if I leave for my world. You have given me the best adventure I could ever have. Thank you, Jason."

"You're welcome, my hero."

"Now let us go home and fix the controller once and for all. I really can't wait to go back to my world. I don't even know what state my world is in right now."

Chapter 9: Stuck Here Forever

When they finally arrived home, Jason was met with a shocker. His parents had returned from their trip.

"Jason, who is this young man?" his mother asked, eyeing Nero's strange attire.

"Err, err," Jason stuttered, "Mom, this is Nero. He's my friend."

"Why is Nero dressed so strangely? He looks vaguely familiar. Do I know him from somewhere?"

"Oh no! You don't. He's a new friend."

"And what is he doing here?"

"He's helping out with my assignment."

"Okay. That's so nice of him," she said, "will Nero be staying for dinner?"

"I don't eat, Mrs Ash," replied Nero.

The woman stared at the game character in confusion.

"He means he's not hungry," Jason quickly chipped in. "We have to go now. I have a very important sum to do. Welcome back, Mom."

"Your father is in the basement."

"I'll see him later. I have something very important to do."

Both Jason and Nero left the living room. The boy locked the door behind him as soon as they stepped into his room.

"Why did you allow my mom to see you?"

Nero frowned, "I don't understand. I was in my invisible mode. You are the only person I permitted to see me. She was not supposed to see me. I'm really confused."

"What do you think is wrong?"

"I think I'm beginning to lose my power. I need to get back to my world as soon as possible or I would be stuck here forever."

"Is it so bad if you're stuck here?"

"That's so selfish of you. If I remain here, my game world will be under grave threat."

"But there are other good fighters in the world. Do you have to be there?"

"Yes I do. I am the one that makes the heroes complete. If I'm not there, there dark side would win over the light side. You don't want that to happen, do you?"

"Okay, let's find a way to get you back."

He reached into his toolbox and extracted a soldering stick. Then he went to the shelf to pick up the controller.

"It's not here," he said.

"What's that?"

"The controller. It's not here. I can't find it."

"Where did you put it?"

"I placed it right here."

"Did your parents take it?"

"Let me ask them."

He left Nero in the room and went to the living room. "Mom, did you enter my room?"

Mrs Ash was sitting behind a laptop and working on a spreadsheet. She looked up at her son and said, "No, I have not been to your room since my return. Is there anything wrong?"

"What about dad? Did he go into my room?"

"Your dad went straight to the basement when we came in" she replied, "are you sure everything is okay?"

Jason gave a false smile. "Everything is fine, Mom. I just felt that someone entered my room in my absence."

"Well, your dad and I did not enter your room."

"Okay, mom. Thanks."

He left her and returned to his room.

"Neither of them took it," he told Nero.

"Without the controller, I won't be able to go home, Jason."

"Don't worry about it. I promise you I'm going to find it. Just calm down. I'm sure it's lying somewhere in the room. I'll find it."

"Have you asked the nanny?"

"The nanny does not enter my room. She is banned from entering. Besides, why would she take a controller in the first place? It could not be the nanny."

For the next thirty minutes, Jason continued to search around his room. He soon grew tired of searching because it was clear that the controller was not in the room. Someone must have taken it.

At the entrance of the house the doorbell rang. Mrs Ash went to answer the door.

"Good afternoon, Mrs Ash," a boy greeted.

"Good afternoon, boy. How may I help you?"

"Is Jason Ash at home, please?"

"Is there anything the matter?"

"My name is Matthew. I'm his schoolmate. I have something important to tell him."

"Okay. Stay put while I go call him."

The woman shut the door and went to knock on her son's door.

"There's someone asking for you at the door."

"Who is the person?"

"He calls himself Matthew. He says he's your friend from school."

"Matt! My bully?" Jason whispered. "What does he want?"

"He says he has something important to tell you. He's waiting for you at the door."

"Okay. Thanks, mom."

Jason stepped out of his room and went to the entrance door. He didn't understand why Matt, one of his greatest enemies, wanted to see him. He thought it must be a different Matt from school. When he opened the door, it was the same Matt who had always been bullying him.

"What do you want, Matt?" Jason asked. He could notice the worried expression on Matt's face.

"I need to tell you something very important."

"I'm listening."

"We stole the controller from your room this morning. Greg and Anderson are planning to use it against you."

Jason frowned. "Use it against me?"

"Yes. They want to power it up so that it could give them extraordinary powers as it gave you. I think you need to stop them. That thing is dangerous. It should not be in the hands of people like Greg and Anderson."

"Why are you helping me," Jason stared at Matt suspiciously.

"I'm sorry for everything I did to you. I just realized that what we had been doing to you all these days were wrong. I wish I could turn back the hands of time and stop all what I did to you. When I realized how determined my friends are about being mean to you, I couldn't stomach it anymore. I have cut off my ties with them."

"Is that why I didn't see you with them when they came to attack me again?"

"Yes. I don't want to associate myself with people like that anymore."

Jason stared at Matt for a moment; he was trying to see whether the boy was telling him the truth or trying to trick him. The expression on Matt's face seemed sincere enough. Besides, if he was trying to deceive them, Nero would find out somehow. He opened the door wider.

"Kindly come in," he told Matt.

The recipient was surprised. "You're inviting me inside?"

"Yes, I want you to meet someone."

He led Matt past the living room to his bedroom. "This is the room we took the controller from," Matt said.

"Yes, this is my room."

"Where is the person you want me to meet?"

"Oh, he's standing by the door."

Matt looked towards the door but didn't see any figure there.

"There's nobody there."

"Look again," said Jason, "He likes doing that."

Matt looked again and saw Nero. He shrank back in fear. "Oh my goodness! Who is this?"

"His name is Nero," explained Jason, "He came from the game world. The controller which you guys stole brought him to our world. He needs to return to his world. If he's not returned as soon as possible, he will be stuck here in our world. We need to help him return to his world."

"Unbelievable!" Matt said in shock, "Is he the person who gave you your power?"

"Yes."

"That's so cool!"

"Oh, he doesn't like the word 'cool'. Use 'boiling' instead."

"Okay. We've got to retrieve that controller. Greg and Anderson think it's going to give them superpowers. We have to stop them before they destroy it."

"Do you know where we can find them?" Nero asked.

"They are either in Greg or Anderson's house."

"We can't go searching for them in both places. There's no time."

"I think they'll be at Greg's. His father is an electrician. He would want to make use of his father's tools."

"Okay. Let's leave immediately."

The three of them trooped out of the room and walked toward the door.

"Where are you headed to, young man?" Jason's father appeared at the door.

"Dad, we have to go and see some of my schoolmates. There's something very important and urgent we have to do."

"Where do these classmates live?"

"They live far away. We need to catch the train before it gets too late."

"Will you be back early for dinner?"

"It depends on how soon we are able to get there?"

"Who is this man dressed so weirdly?"

"This is Nero, Dad. He's my friend," said Jason, he placed his hand on Matt's shoulder, "and this is Matthew. He's also my friend. We want to go and rescue another friend."

Mr Ash stared at Nero and Matt and asked "can your friend drive?"

"Who? Nero?"

"Yes."

"I don't know. I really don't know," he turned to Nero "Can you drive?"

"I can definitely drive a car."

"Then you don't have to take the train," said Mr Ash. "You can get there faster in my car." He threw his car key at Nero who caught it in the air.

"Thank you dad. You're the best."

"You better be back before nightfall," the man told his son. He turned to Nero and said, "Bring my son back home safely."

"No harm will come to him."

The three entered the car and Nero zoomed away.

"Have you ever driven a car before?"

Nero shook his head. "No, but I have read an article about how to drive a car. It's pretty easy."

"You're doing amazingly great for a first-timer."

"Beginner's luck, I guess."

"Matt, you will have to give Nero the right directions to take. Time is not on our side. We have to be as fast as possible."

While Nero drove on, Matt gave him directions to take.

"After you leave, will you ever come back again?" Matt asked Nero.

"I don't think I would. There's nothing for me to come and do here. My job is done in this world. Jason brought me here for a reason. The reason was to stop bullying. I'm glad you have realized that it is not nice to bully other people. This world would be a lot better if people learn how to respect one another. Nobody has the right to bully another; the effects can be quite traumatic. It can often upset the victim's bright future. The school is supposed to be an institution for learning things, not for being victimized."

"I hope Greg and Anderson have a change of heart," Matt said, "They are actually nice if they choose not to bully people. I wish I could continue my friendship with them; only if they are willing to change for the best."

"Nobody is beyond redemption" said Nero, "Anyone can be saved. I am sure that they will come around and become better people. Besides, I scared them real good the first time I met them!"

"You have met them?"

Nero nodded. "They had come to get Jason again. I had to show them that Jason is not someone they can bully. They have a great gift but they don't know it. If they could channel the energy they have into doing good things, they would be a lot happier. Their parents would be proud of them. The society would be proud of them. Everybody has a gift, but bullying is not one of those gifts. The earlier they stop, the better it would be for them."

"We're almost getting there," Matt said. "Turn left into this street. Greg's house is the fourth house to the right. It's easy to locate."

"Remember," said Jason, "The controller is the priority. We have to retrieve it from them by all means. And it must not be damaged."

"I think you should let me approach them first," Matt suggested. "They would let down their guards when they see me. I'll try to reason with them."

"What if they don't listen to you?"

"Then both of you can come in. Either way, we're getting the controller from them."

Chapter 10: Become Superheroes And Make This World A Better Place

Greg had just finished soldering the controller when Matt stepped in.

"What are you doing here?" Anderson asked, "I thought you had nothing to do with someone like us anymore."

"You have to stop this," said Matt. "What you're doing is wrong."

"How is it wrong?" asked Greg. "We just want to gain superpowers. We're not hurting anybody."

"But you plan to hurt Jason with your power. What has the boy done to you? I think you should stop this."

"We are not planning to hurt the boy," answered Greg, "We just want to repair the controller and gain power from it."

"What are you going to do with the superpower when you have it?"

"We want to change the world," said Anderson, "We want to become superheroes. We saw Jason's superhero. Jason has proved to us that superheroes are real. We just want to become superheroes and make this world a better place."

"You can't make the world a better place by bullying other people."

"You're right. We regret our past. We are looking for a way to correct all the wrong things we have done. It has taken you and Jason with his protector to show us that we are the villains. We don't like being the bad guys. We want to be on the side of the good guys. If we become superheroes, we will stop every other bad guy in our neighborhood."

Matt stared at them. "This sounds suspicious."

"I know you'll find it hard to believe us, but everything we just told you is true. You see, something happened to us this afternoon. We thought we were goners when that huge superhero man grabbed us by the collars. But he didn't hurt us. He was compassionate. If someone who is a lot more powerful than us can be compassionate, then why can't we be accommodating of our neighbors?"

"What would you do if Jason appeared here right now?" Matt asked.

"We would ask for his forgiveness. We have done terrible things to that boy. I hope he is kind enough to forgive us. We have been cruel and self-centered."

Matt left them and returned to Jason and Nero. "I think it's time for you to come in. I can't believe what I'm witnessing."

"What's going on?" asked Jason.

"I think it's better you both see it yourself."

Jason and Nero got out of the car and stepped into the house. Jason took careful steps towards Greg and Anderson.

"Hello guys," he said awkwardly.

"Hello Jason," said the boys in unison.

"What are you guys doing?"

Greg and Anderson stared at each other and said, "We have fixed the controller. We are sorry we stole it from your room. You can have it back. It's wrong for us to take it without your consent. We thought it would give us superpowers just like it gave you."

They handed the controller to Jason.

"It's not the controller that gave me the power," Jason explained. "It's Nero who give me the power."

"It's the man who gave you the power?"

Jason nodded.

"How is that possible?"

"Nero is not from this world. He came from my video game world. It's hard to believe, but it's true. When I plugged this controller into my game, there was a spark of lightning, then Nero appeared. He's my favorite character from the game."

"What's the name of the game?"

"Power Wolf Heroes."

"That's incredible," said Greg.

"Now Nero needs to return to the game world. He's already losing his power. If I don't return him today, then he will be stuck here forever. He has come to this world to help me. He made me believe in myself. Now I'm not scared of anything anymore. No offense, but none of you scare me anymore, either I am powerful or I am not. I will never be a victim of bullying again. All I have to do is believe in myself. Victims of bullying are often people with low self-confidence. They are the ones that feel fear often."

"How can we help Nero return to his world?" asked Anderson.

"You have already helped him," said Jason. "You already fixed the broken controller. What I need to do now is to take him back to my house and connect the controller back to my game. I'm sure that's how to return him to his world."

"We are so sorry for keeping you waiting for so long," Greg told Nero.

"It's fine, Greg," answered Nero. "In your world, everything happens for a reason. That's not how things work in my own world. There is no pattern. All we know in my world is to constantly fight enemies. We either win, or we lose. But we don't stay in game over forever. Unlike this world, we can come back to life as many times as possible."

"I think your world is a lot better than ours," said Anderson, "I would like to live in a world where I had infinite lives. I would be able to wake up anytime I wanted and not go to school. Can you take me to your world?"

"Just like I can't feel at home here, you will never feel at home in my world. In my world, we know only one thing, and that is to fight until we get game over. We live to fight battles until we get another game over. Then we live again and fight again. That's the routine. We don't do anything else. Everything in my world is based around fighting battles. You won't thrive in my world. You should stick to your world of peace. Your life here has purpose. You can enjoy food. You can play games. You make friends. You can be with your family. You can learn new things. There is no limit to the things you can benefit from in this world. Do not yearn for my kind of world. After some time, either you are the winner, or the vanquished. You will get tired of the constant battles. You will wish for a brief moment of peace, but you won't find it in my world. In my world, every character is programmed to battle for all of eternity."

"I think it's time for me to take you back to my room" said Jason.

"Can we follow you?" asked Greg. "We also want to see Nero off."

"Of course you can," said Jason smiling. He turned to Nero, "Why don't you show them the fire?"

"What fire?" the boys were confused.

"Nero can produce fire from any part of his body."

"Wow! That's amazing!"

"Show them, Nero."

"Okay."

Nero flicked his fingers and fire danced on his palms. The boys stared mesmerized at the magic they had just witnessed.

"Throw it like you do in the game, Nero."

The superhero merged the two fireballs together and they formed a bigger flame. Then, he hurled it far away from them. The boys watched in wonder as the fire travelled in the air and landed on a plain field, causing a huge explosion. Then the fire disappeared suddenly.

"Where did the fire go?" Matt asked.

"I made it go out," answered Nero.

"Wow! You can put out fire remotely?"

Nero smiled for the first time. "I guess I would make a good fireman if I was a human being."

All the boys laughed.

They all returned to the car and Nero drove them back to Jason's house. Mr and Mrs Ash were surprised that Jason came back with two more friends.

"What's the occasion, son?" asked Mr Ash, "Are you guys having a party or what?"

"Thanks for the ride, Dad." He returned his car keys and ushered the rest of his friends into the house, up the stairs, and into his room.

"Is anyone here entering this room for the first time?" he asked.

Matt, Greg and Anderson smiled. It was a good joke.

"This is the moment," said Jason, locking the door behind them.

"Why are you locking the door?" Matt asked.

"There is going to be a massive bolt of lightning. I don't want my parents stepping in at that moment.

"Are we safe," Matt asked worriedly.

"We're all absolutely safe."

He crossed the room and switched on his television. Then he switched on the game. As he was about to plug in the controller, Nero said:

"Wait, Jason."

"What's the matter, Nero."

"I need to say my goodbyes. Jason, you have been a very good friend. I am glad I came to your world. If I have the ability, I will explain to the other heroes of Power Wolf. I'm sure they'll all be proud of you. Whenever you play the game, I will always remember you as I fight my enemies." And without seeking for permission, he drew Jason close to himself and hugged him. Jason was initially scared. He had expected to be jolted by electricity but he wasn't.

Nero turned to the other three boys, "I am glad you boys are now better people. Remember, bullying is never right. Say NO to bullying. Whenever you see anyone being bullied, you should always help the victim and tell an adult. Teach the person to be confident in themselves. You don't have to possess superpowers to become superheroes; you are superheroes by the decisions you make. Fight against bullying and the world will thank you." He hugged them one after the other.

"One other thing, Jason. Your wish will come true. It is your wish that will take me home. When you plug in the controller, don't forget to wish that I was back in my world. That is the only thing that will work. If you don't wish that, I will be stuck here and more superheroes from the game would appear. You really don't want that."

"Okay, I understand what you mean."

Jason reluctantly plugged the controller to the game with tears in his eyes. Immediately, a bright sparkle appeared from the game. It was a blinding blue light that got every one of them screaming in shock! Blue lightning filled the entire room. Jason watched as the lightning circled around Nero. It covered him entirely. Then it returned into a little hole in the game cartridge where it had come from. The lightning had taken Nero with it.

Then everywhere became silent again, until there was a loud bang on the door. Jason's parents were screaming his name from the corridor. He went to the door and opened it.

"What's wrong, Dad?"

"What's going on in this room?" I thought I saw something that looked like a bright light.

"Oh, that's the movie from the television. Everything is fine, Dad. You don't have to worry."

The man stepped into the room. "Where is your big friend?"

"You mean Nero? He left. Didn't you see him when he was leaving?"

"The man looked confused. "He left? I didn't see him leave. Anyway, be careful. Don't burn the house down." He left the room.

Jason locked the door again.

"Now, what are we going to do about the controller?" Greg asked.

"We return it to the store."

"I don't think that's good enough. What if someone else comes across it?" said Anderson.

"Why don't you keep it here in your room? You'll safeguard it. That way no one is going to use it wrongly."

"No, it can't be in my room. I may be tempted to use it again when I miss Nero."

"The solution is easy," said Matt. "I will keep the controller. I don't have the game, so there's no way for me to use it. If I don't have the game and you don't have the controller, then there's no way both of them will meet."

"That's a good plan."

"Thank you, guys, for your support," Jason said sincerely.

"You don't have to thank us," said Greg, "Friends are supposed to always support each other."

They all laughed. Jason could not believe that he was now friends with his former enemies.

There was a knock on the door.

"Dinner is ready, boys," Mrs Ash spoke from downstairs. "Oh, and Jason… there is a young lady here to see you. She says her name is Emily."

GAME OVER

(The End)

Book 2 - A Video Game Story 2: Trapped on Battle Royale Island

Dan Ashcraft

Table Of Contents

Chapter 1: Nothing Changes.. 1

Chapter 2: One Ticket to Nowhere, Please 6

Chapter 3: A Mysterious Island 9

Chapter 4: Three Wizards 14

Chapter 5: Team Up! 17

Chapter 6: Switching Sides 21

Chapter 7: Game On! 25

Chapter 8: It's a Battle Royale! 31

Chapter 9: Everything Gets a Little Crazy 35

Chapter 10: Nero Loses?! 37

Chapter 11: Last Man Standing 40

Chapter 12: Victory Royale 43

Chapter 13: Continue? 45

Free Bonus! 51

Chapter 1: Nothing Changes

"Jason, come get breakfast before it gets cold!" called Mrs. Thandie from downstairs.

My parents were away for a week because of work. Mrs. Thandie took care of the house and cooked most of my meals for me since I wasn't allowed to use the kitchen unless it was to make myself a sandwich.

It had been several months since the last time I had skipped school. I used to try and avoid going to school and ended up being late a lot of the time because the bullies wouldn't leave me alone. They had made my life horrible, and every moment I was forced to be there had made me completely miserable.

I finished my game of Power Wolf Heroes and whispered, "Awesome job, Nero! You rock!" I had played Power Wolf Heroes nearly every afternoon and every morning, but I still hadn't gotten bored of it. It was what had often distracted me and made me late to school. Now, however, I played only if I knew I would have enough time. I didn't want to miss the time I spent on the bus with my friends.

I switched off the console and went downstairs. I was happier than I had ever been, and it was all thanks to my newfound friends. Emily sent me a text to remind me that the bus was around the corner from my house. She sent me a message every morning now to make sure that I didn't miss my bus and have to walk to school. I used to get so caught up in my video games that I lost track of time and ended up walking to school *a lot*.

I waited outside for the bus while still chewing on the last bit of my pancake, humming the music from the game. Mrs. Thandie's pancakes were the best, I thought. Even better than my mom's. My mom wasn't home that often, but she did enjoy cooking my favorite things when she was around.

"Emily!" I called as I stepped onto the bus and waved excitedly. Her smile when she saw me made me stumble a little. We were becoming really good friends, and I got butterflies in my stomach every time I saw her. I tried to seem confident even though I felt completely shaky and shy on the inside. Nero had returned to his home in Power Wolf Heroes three months ago. It was because of him that I had three best friends now. He had helped me become more confident, and my bullies stopped being so horrible to me.

Matt, Greg, and Anderson had learned their lesson and wanted to try to be nicer people. The first few days were a little awkward at school, but Matt helped everyone get on board. Emily saw the change in me and was very happy that I wasn't withdrawn and moody with everyone anymore. She got along with everyone, even the ever-prickly Greg, who still struggled to keep his mean words to himself.

"I saved you a seat!" Emily said happily as I reached her seat in the back of the bus. Next to her was Matt, who greeted me with a nod. Greg and Anderson sat one row in front of us and leaned over the backs of their seats to talk to us. I joined them, ignoring the stink eye I was getting from Brian as I sat down next to Emily.

"How was your weekend?" she asked.

I immediately told her about my Saturday. Emily had been at her grandmother's over the weekend, so she didn't have time to come over for a visit. The boys and I ended up sleeping over at a different person's house every night because there were just too many things we wanted to do or try.

"Then we went over to that game shop –"

"The one down by the tracks? The one that has been closed for like six months?" Emily interrupted, frowning.

"Yeah," I said excitedly, "how do you know about that game shop?"

"You told me, remember. It's where you found that weird diamond controller," Emily reminded me. "You said you wouldn't go back there again, though."

"Oh that's right," Greg said, "Emily had dinner with all of us after we fixed it and Nero left."

Anderson and Matt smiled, "Yeah, that was a pretty fun day, even if it didn't really start out the best way."

"Wait, you went over to Jason's house?" Brian said angrily, interrupting our conversation.

Emily smiled awkwardly, "Yes, Brian, we're friends, and we all had dinner with his parents. We visit there almost every weekend."

"Why would you even –"

"Stop it, Brian," Matt said.

Brian's face turned beet red. Normally, Matt and the others would have joined in on his teasing and bullying, but since three months ago, we had become best friends. Brian was only brave when he was being mean to me or the other boys in our grade. He would never go against any of the older kids in the higher grades.

I grinned at Brian as he looked ready to explode from anger. He glared at me, then at Matt and the others, and then sat down in his seat in a huff.

"Thanks, Matt," I said politely. I was very happy that Brian had left me alone, but Matt, Greg, and Anderson weren't going to be around all the time. I could see by the way Brian kept glancing at Emily that he thought she should be sitting with him instead. He did a rather good job of ignoring the rest of us. It was fine by me, I thought.

"Did you guys put the controller in a safe place?" Emily asked, talking a little lower so that none of the other children overheard.

"Yeah, Matt's got it locked up at his house."

"Is it a good idea to have it just lying around?" Emily asked, her eyes wide.

"Oh, my parents don't really touch my stuff, and anyway, I keep it in a shoebox in my treehouse," Matt said, a little proud of himself.

"It doesn't sound very safe," Emily said and sat back, folding her arms across her chest. "What if it rains?"

"Emily's right, though," I said.

Matt looked thoughtfully at the both of us, "It's safe for now, but I'll see if I can find a new place for it. My dad should be able to help."

We talked a little more on how we managed to fix the controller and everything else that had happened around that time. We all laughed, especially when Matt recounted my Nero-like powers as I flicked him six feet through the air. There weren't any hard feelings anymore, and my powers didn't last long anyway.

"Do you guys want to come over this weekend again to play Power Wolf Heroes?" I asked.

"Sure!" everyone agreed.

"Why don't we plan something for summer break, too? We can take turns staying over at each other's houses," Greg offered.

For the rest of the ride to school we chatted happily about our plans and what activities we were going to do.

***

The school day had ended at least fifteen minutes ago, but I had gotten distracted with the new video game character I was designing. I had just finished with the outfit he was going to wear and was busy planning what the character's moves and weapons were going to be.

My thoughts were rudely interrupted when I walked straight into Brian.

"You missed your bus, Jason," Brian said, making himself look bigger than he really was. He pulled his shoulders back and stood taller than me.

"Leave me alone, Brian," I said, rolling my eyes at him. Of course he had waited until the hallway was clear before targeting me. He usually only picked on me on the bus before school, but I guess since Emily was now my friend he couldn't do it in front of her without looking bad.

"Why are you in such a rush, Jason? Want to go home and play your stupid games?" Brian smiled like he just told the funniest joke in the world.

"Why can't you just leave me alone?" I said angrily.

"Because you won't let me be friends with Emily!"

"She makes her own choices, Brian! She is only too polite to completely tell you off," I added, getting annoyed now.

"No, she's only that way because of you!" Brian hissed.

I shook my head and tried to push past him. He got even angrier and shoved me, making me fall hard. My backpack slid across the walkway.

"You think you're so brave, Jason, but you're just a wimp with big friends." Brian stomped on my backpack in anger and kicked it for good measure.

"You're just a bully, Brian, it's no wonder you don't have any friends," I said snidely. As soon as the words left my mouth I felt bad. Nero wouldn't approve of my attitude, and I knew my words were rude, but I was tired of him being mean to me all the time just because Emily and I were friends now.

Brian's face grew even redder, and he stormed off, kicking my backpack as hard as he could against the wall. I remained where I was for a few heartbeats, waiting for him to come back and kick me like he kicked my backpack. He didn't.

I finally made it to the bus stop after checking that all my stuff was still in one piece. I lost a few pencils, but I could still use them later if I sharpened the broken end.

Emily was there waiting for me, swinging her legs on the bench, staring at the little stones she was kicking around with her sneakers.

"Hi, Emily," I said quietly.

As soon as she heard me she stood up and turned to face me, "What's wrong? Where were you?"

"Brian cornered me outside my class."

"What do you mean?" she asked, frowning at me and looking like she didn't believe me.

"Emily, he's a bully. He stopped me in the hall and threw my bag around."

Emily chewed on the inside of her cheek, looking down at her shoes. She said nothing.

"Let's go home," I said.

We walked in silence. It was a little awkward because of my bringing up what Brian had done. I knew that for whatever reason Emily still liked talking to him.

"Why do you still talk to him?" I asked. Emily was kind and wanted to be friendly with everyone, but kids like Brian only made trouble.

"He's not really a bad person," Emily said.

"Are you sure?" I snorted.

"Jason," Emily scolded me, "Brian and I aren't really *friends*, but I still talk to him."

"But why?"

Emily shrugged, "He seems like he wants to be friends. Sometimes it's all people really want." Emily smiled and bumped into me gently to prove her point.

Chapter 2: One Ticket to Nowhere, Please

Brian was furious. He couldn't punch Jason in his big, geeky face, no matter how much he wanted to. His mom would completely lose her mind if he did. He had already gotten into trouble once for hitting another kid, and he didn't want to have to change schools again. It was hard to make friends in a new school, and besides, Emily was in *this* one.

He just wanted Emily to like him more than she seemed to like Jason.

Why was it so hard?

Brian had overheard the boys talking about some stupid video game and wondered why anyone would even play something that no one seemed to have heard about. He certainly hadn't heard about it, and his dad let him test a lot of the new games that came out. It was one of the things he was good at. No one could beat him in any game that he played, and it made him feel powerful.

Brian was still fuming when he got home. His mom didn't bother asking why he was late and only asked if he had finished his homework.

"I'm going to my room," Brian grumbled.

"What about dinner?" his mom asked. "I made spaghetti. It's your favorite."

"I'm not hungry." It wasn't really the truth, but he was too angry to eat anything now anyway. He had already started planning his revenge.

"I'll get back at them. I'll show them," Brian said and smiled smugly to himself, "And I know exactly how."

As he watched Jason and Matt get off the bus at Jason's house the next day, Brian set his plan into motion. Instead of getting off at his own stop, he got off at Matt's house instead. He made sure no one on the bus saw him walk to Matt's front door.

It was too early for Matt's parents to be home already, but Brian wanted to be sure that no one would catch him. He jumped the fence and jiggled the back door handle. The neighborhood was small enough that almost everyone knew each other and there were rarely any break-ins, so people either forgot to lock their doors or just chose to leave them unlocked.

Brian knew Matt didn't have any pets either, so he felt confident that he was safe for now.

Brian had no idea where Matt's room was, so he searched the whole house until he found a room that looked like it could belong to him. Nope, it was his brother's room. Brian didn't know a whole lot about Matt, but he thought the boy was an only child like him. Huh, who knew?

Brian left the room untouched and found one that looked like it had been used more recently and was definitely a lot messier than the brother's. Matt hadn't made the bed this morning, and there were still random clothes scattered about the room. He carefully stepped over the mess and started rummaging through the bottom of Matt's closet for the shoebox in question. None of the shoeboxes held the controller, though, and Brian was starting to become angry and frustrated.

"He said it was in the closet, didn't he? Or did I just imagine that part?" Brian asked as he stared into the messy black hole that was a teenage boy's closet of clothes. He began second-guessing himself. He was so sure that he had heard them talking about keeping it in a shoebox! Where else would he keep a shoebox except in his closet somewhere?

Brian pulled the desk chair closer, stood on it as it wobbled dangerously and peered into the top of the closet. Still nothing. Brian carefully replaced the desk chair where he found it and stood in the middle of the room and looked around, scratching his head. There! His eyes landed on the tree house outside Matt's window. That was the only place it could possibly still be, Brian thought.

He sprinted outside and climbed up the planks that were nailed to the base of the tree as fast as he could.

"Whoa!" Brian exclaimed when he lifted the lid. It looked so much cooler than he had imagined. For a very brief moment he considered keeping it for himself, but he didn't want to be caught with it in his possession. It would mean being shipped off to a whole new school. Brian stuffed the controller into his pocket and closed the lid on the shoebox.

"Phase one, complete." Brian grinned as he hopped the fence again and jogged the rest of the way home.

Over the following days, Brian watched and listened closely. He sat close to their group on the bus and made mental notes. Brian still greeted Emily every morning, but he did, for the most part, try to ignore Jason. He needed to get into Jason's house, but he didn't think it was going to be as easy as it had been at Matt's.

He would have to pick a day that Jason would go to one of his friend's houses instead. He knew that Jason's parents had a housekeeper, too. It made things complicated, but not very difficult. He would simply have to be smarter and quicker.

"Time for phase two," he said as he got off the bus alone.

**

Brian had come up with this brilliant idea to ship the game and the controller to an imaginary place. At least, he thought it was a brilliant idea. He knew Matt and Jason would be upset if they couldn't find their precious items. Brian laughed quietly to himself as he filled out the shipping label to Island 24B, Delta Coast, South Pacific and stuck the stamps carefully in the top right corner.

Brian laughed again, feeling very proud of his scheme, "Like anyone would actually believe that place is real. But at least it should take a very long time before the game and that controller made their way back to Nebraska."

***

"I haven't been able to find my game," Jason said as the group crowded into his room, sitting on the end of Jason's bed. Some of them took up their usual spots on the floor as they talked about what could have happened to it.

Jason heard a low whistle and looked around his room. Nobody else seemed to notice the noise at first, and then they all looked at each other with concern.

Brian had heard it, too.

"Do you guys hear that, or am I going crazy?" Greg asked.

"Wait I hear it too," Emily said and everything around them seemed to be getting fuzzy around the edges. Brian held his breath and felt uneasy as his ears popped.

"Is-is that wind?" he heard Anderson ask. "It sounds like we're in the middle of a storm."

Brian felt his stomach drop. It was the same feeling he got when he was on a rollercoaster and it had just gone over the edge, plummeting down to the ground.

He looked down at his feet, and he could see nothing but clouds and blue sky. Brian had to keep himself from shouting in fear as the ground came rushing closer and closer—faster than any rollercoaster he had ever been on.

Chapter 3: A Mysterious Island

"Hi, Benny!" Rory called as he leaned into the sorting room at the doorway.

"Morning, Champ!" Benny called back. Everyone at the Post Office called him Champ. His dad worked here and always bragged to his colleagues about him.

"Anything good?" Rory asked. It was very rare that a package came in with no recipient name listed. When that did happen, though, the package got separated from the main sorting area and placed in a holding area for a while to see if anyone contacted them regarding the package in question.

Naturally, if no one came calling, after a couple of weeks, the package was opened and the contents claimed by the Post Office. Once, Rory got to keep a cool pair of sunglasses, but mostly what was left here was junk. Sweaters, socks, a letter or two from people who probably mistyped the address—junk.

"The usual!" Benny said, "I think your dad did save something for you that came in a while ago. Check with him."

"Awesome!" Rory zipped through the sorting room straight to the back office where his dad was already hard at work. As soon as he stepped through the door, his dad tossed a padded mail bag at him.

"I saved this one for you. I think you'll like it." His dad gave him a happy smile.

"Thanks, dad! I'll heat up leftovers for lunch! See you at home for dinner!"

***

"Alright, guys, let's end the game quickly. I've got some things to do," Rory said into his headset. His friends complained in his ears, but he ignored them. He made his character do a backflip and while he was still hanging in the air, he used his plasma rifle to defeat the last enemy on the map, ending the match with style.

"Booyah!" he shouted as the game's victory screen showed his team and each person's score. "I'll be back in a flash," Rory said and muted his mic before flinging it onto his chair with a quick flick of his wrist.

He stomped down the hall in his socks and rubbed his pup's ears as he took the stairs two by two in a rush to get to the kitchen.

As he opened the fridge to check for leftovers, his eyes fell on the package that he had left on the kitchen table. He wasn't too excited. Rory expected it to be another book—his dad liked to save those especially for him. He could see that his dad had already opened the package, but Rory couldn't see inside.

Rory grabbed a soda from the fridge and ran back up the stairs to his room, the package now tucked under his arm. His golden retriever pup, Ben, just wagged his tail happily as he passed him at the top of the stairs.

Rory popped the disk into one of his older gaming consoles and read the back of the case while the system started up. Upbeat music blasted from his speakers as the screen came to life.

There was a very strong-looking character on the main menu screen that bounced around just like they did in other fighting games that Rory had played before. Rory grimaced. "The graphics don't look too cool," he said to himself.

Rory looked at the controller still wrapped in bubble wrap inside the package and carefully unwrapped it. The moment he touched it, he felt a slight electrical shock. It wasn't very strong, but it made Rory feel as though there was definitely something special about this particular controller.

He plugged it into the console, and the controller came to life. Lightning sparked and zoomed around, casting a bright blue glow around the room.

"Awesome," Rory said and plopped down in his chair, starting a new game. He looked at the names below every character. He could only guess at their powers, so he picked the one that looked the coolest. It was a red-haired character that wore golden cuffs and dark-red pants.

"He looks cool," Rory said to himself and scrolled through the character menu, looking at everything the game had to offer. There was a Story Mode that Rory was interested in, but he would play that one a bit later, he thought to himself.

Rory played for hours, trying out every single character. He liked Mertini the most because he had the coolest moves. The dancing fighter's style and speed made him very hard to hit for any of the others, except Nero. Rory realized that Nero was the leader of the group of fighters, so it made sense that he was the strongest.

"Rory!" His mom's loud voice suddenly made him jump guiltily in his seat. The movement made him jerk the cable of the controller clear from the socket. The console's warning bell reminded him to plug the controller back in. Unlike the more modern games, this one didn't pause when the controller disconnected, and it made Rory panic a little—he was in the middle of the final match! He fumbled with the controller and dropped it on his foot.

Rory tried to pull his foot out of the way but only succeeded in kicking the controller hard up into the air. He bounced on one foot, mumbled angry words under his breath, and watched as it bounced, rolled, and skidded across his bedroom floor and out the door. He watched in horror as it slid to a stop at the top of the stairs in front of Ben's twitching nose.

"Ben! No!" Rory shouted, but it was too late. The lump of a golden retriever bounded excitedly towards it, scooped it up with its slobbery jaws, and ran as fast as it could away from Rory.

As Ben bit down hard on the controller, sparks started to fill the room. They grew in intensity and turned into a blindingly bright light that seemed to fill the whole house. When Rory was able to open his eyes again, there was nothing new that he could immediately see.

"What on earth was that?" Rory asked, shocked at the sudden blinding light. For all the flash and spark, there was nothing more to show. Rory was glad that he hadn't been electrocuted.

Rory sighed and hung his head just as a voice behind him spoke, "Who are you?"

"Oh dear," the stranger said quietly as Rory followed after the playful dog. It took a few tries and a lot of persuasion, but Rory eventually got the controller away from Ben. (He had to trade a whole lot of snacks and belly rubs!)

Rory stood there like an idiot. His brain was not catching up fast enough.

"Who? What? How?" Rory mumbled. He took a deep breath and finally turned to look at the strange man that had appeared in his bedroom. His hair was a bright red that looked like burning fire. It even moved a little like fire, but Rory thought that was probably just a trick of the light.

He looked like a character in a fighting type of video game. He had lots of muscles and an awesome-looking outfit. He looked familiar, as if Rory had seen him before, but couldn't quite place him.

The stranger had thick, golden cuffs around his wrist that also looked as though there was a fire burning on the surface. His pants were thick and a deep, dark red.

"I'm Nero, and your dog just ate my ticket home."

***

"I'm sorry about your controller," Rory said as he held up the mangled pieces of the controller. The spark of lightning that was inside was now completely dead. The case was cracked and chewed on, and the analog sticks were gone. They were probably somewhere in the garden. He had gone after Ben as fast as he could, but the pup was eager to play and had a good minute head start.

Nero looked on in disappointment.

"Look, it was an accident. You came out of nowhere and –"

"Not nowhere. I come from the world of Power Wolf Heroes."

"That retro game I found?"

"Found?"

"Yeah, someone sent it in the mail. It ended in the lost and found because no one claimed it." Rory indicated the bag that held only the bubblewrap now.

Nero inspected the bag and saw the postmark.

"Did Jason send this?" Nero asked.

"Who's Jason?" Rory was more confused than ever. There was this strange-looking guy in his bedroom that just appeared out of the video game. Now he was asking about some other person as if he was supposed to know everything.

"The boy who gave you this game. Where is he?"

"I don't know a Jason, dude. The package was delivered anonymously from somewhere else in the world." Rory said.

"Nebraska," Nero nodded.

"Yeah, that place. But I swear, I don't know who sent it or how it got here. All I know is that my dad found it in the lost and found thing at the Post Office and gave it to me."

Nero paced the room, and Rory stood to the side watching his every move. His toe still hurt from where the controller had hit it, and his brain was running laps in his skull trying not to freak out completely.

"You're from inside the game?" Rory asked carefully.

"Yes."

"How did you get here?"

"The controller. It's magical, and it can call me from within the game and bring me into this world," Nero said.

"Like a portal?"

Nero frowned for a brief moment, then recalled something he had read on Jason's computer the last time he had been in his world. "Yes, exactly. I was pulled here through the portal the controller created."

"Okay, how do I send you back?" Rory asked.

"With the controller."

"But it's completely wrecked!"

"Yes, it is."

"Then, how?" Rory asked, finally annoyed at the mysterious stranger.

"Fix it," Nero said matter-of-factly.

"Fix it? You think it's that simple?"

"Yes."

"How? I don't know anything about electronics. Besides, you'll need three wishes just to put it together again. Never mind getting it to work again."

"Is there such a place here that can grant us wishes?"

Rory squinted disbelievingly at Nero. Was he serious? Rory was about to tell him off when a thought occurred to him, "There is one place that we could take it to."

Chapter 4: Three Wizards

"We only serve the Masters."

"What?" Nero asked. The Wizard in dark blue robes answered him again in the same monotone voice.

"But we need –," Nero and Rory started talking at once. The wizard held his hand up, and the two of them fell silent.

"We only serve the Masters."

Rory pulled a funny face as the wizard repeated himself for the second time.

"What does that mean?" Nero asked, feeling the little bit of hope he had drifting away.

"It means," Rory said, "that they can't help us –"

"Well, that's just perfect!" Nero said and sighed.

"Until we can defeat the teams in the Battle Royale Arena and become Battle Masters."

"Battle… Masters?" Nero looked at Rory with the same stupid expression that the boy had had on his face when Nero appeared out of nowhere.

"Here on Wipeout Island we spend our days training and fighting in Battle Arenas. When we defeat all the teams and end up with the highest number of knockouts compared to the other teams, we win and become Battle Masters."

"What are so special about Battle Masters?" Nero asked.

"We only serve the Masters," the three wizards said in unison and then waved their hands at the door, indicating that they were done talking to them.

"They are treated like celebrities, or like royalty," Rory explained.

"And in order to become a Master, we have to win?" Nero asked.

Rory nodded, "There can be only one winning team. There was that one year where there were two. They ended up making a pact to take out the other teams first and finished in a clear tie."

"How does a tie happen? Even if two are left standing with an even amount of knockouts, only one of them will be able to be the winner," Nero said, frowning.

"Normally that is how it works," Rory agreed, "but the team that won was in the lead by one point when they fired the winning shot."

Nero looked horror struck, "Winning shot? You shoot people here?"

"For fun, yes."

The only reference Nero had for that was through the research he had done at Jason's house all those months ago. The articles he had found did not paint a fun picture.

"Wait, wait, aren't you concerned for the well-being of those who play the game," Nero said. "How dangerous is it here?"

Rory laughed out loud and dragged Nero out of the Wizards 'hut.

"What is so amusing?" Nero asked, shocked.

Rory placed a firm and comforting hand on Nero's shoulder, "No one dies on the island, Nero. We're not a bunch of barbarians."

"The losers just get knocked out, and they are then removed from the game," Rory finished explaining.

Relief flooded through Nero, "That makes so much more sense."

Again Rory laughed, "You really are strange!"

Rory carefully rewrapped the controller in the old t-shirt and stuffed it back into his backpack.

"What do we do now, Rory?" Nero asked as they picked their way through the streets back to Rory's house. On nearly every surface and stuck on every lamppost were posters of the upcoming Battle Royale.

"We have to make a team of seven people in order to qualify to take part in the Battle Royale," Rory said.

"Is it hard to find people to team up with?"

"No, not at all," Rory said but hesitated for a moment before continuing. "But, my usual team is already full. I wasn't planning on participating this season."

Nero remained quiet and Rory left him to his thoughts as they arrived at his house. Rory gently put the backpack in the corner of his room and left the pieces of the controller inside. He still felt completely horrible for destroying it and getting Nero stuck in the human world.

"We can find people who would be willing to join our team," Rory said.

"Our team?"

"Yeah, you and me. I figured, since you're already here, you could be part of the Battle Royale Event. I can ask some of my friends to join us. I should be able to get a team together," Rory said a little distractedly.

"Friends?" Nero asked. A light went on in his eyes as Rory watched, and Nero clapped his hands together excitedly.

"What? What is it?" Rory asked, getting to his feet.

Nero held his hands out in front of him, and Rory saw a bunch of little orange sparks light up at his fingertips.

"Don't burn my house down!" Rory said, alarmed. "All I said was we need more people."

"I know," Nero said. "I'm bringing my friends here." Nero closed his eyes, and a light wind began blowing inside the house. Rory stepped back into the doorway of his room, keeping his distance from whatever it was that Nero was doing.

The wind began growing in strength and speed, making the windows rattle and loose bits of paper spin around the room.

Rory held his hand up to his face as he squinted. He could barely see Nero through the clouds and wall of wind that was beginning to form in the room. As he watched, blurry shapes began to take form inside the whirlwind. Soon enough, those blurry shapes began to take the forms of people. Kids, like himself, Rory noted.

Rory blinked once, then twice, and when the wind finally died down, there were six people standing in his room.

Chapter 5: Team Up!

The ground rushed up to meet us, and I held my breath, feeling as though my heart was going to explode. I blinked, and when I opened my eyes again, we were much, much closer to the ground than I had expected. I squeezed my eyes shut and braced myself.

We didn't hit the ground, even though it felt like we would at any second. Instead the ground suddenly just appeared beneath my feet as if it had been there all along. There was a gasp from Emily, and I realized that I wasn't alone.

I glanced around and saw that we were all still together.

"What was that?" Greg asked, looking a little green.

"I don't know," I said, standing as still as possible until the world stopped spinning.

We were standing in a fairly large room. It looked like some kid's bedroom, though much bigger than any I had ever seen.

I didn't know how we got here, but I was sure that we weren't in Nebraska anymore. For one thing, I could hear the ocean not too far away. For another, I could tell by the looks on everyone's face that they thought the same thing. What annoyed me even more was that Brian was standing here with us, looking as confused as the rest of us.

There was an empty bag by my feet, and I picked it up.

"Island Twenty-Four B, Delta Coast, South Pacific," I read out loud. I didn't recognize the address, but I could clearly read the Nebraska post mark in the corner.

"Where on earth are we?" Anderson asked. "And how did we get here?"

"I made this place up!" Brian half shouted and half laughed. "It's not real! It can't be!" He continued to turn in circles and then ran to the window as if he would see something to prove that this must have been a prank.

"Then you have a powerful imagination, bro, because I'm seeing this, too," Greg mocked.

"Greg, be nice," I said to remind him. He was a good guy now, but he still had a lot of the old snippy, mean part in him that he couldn't help but let out once in a while. Sometimes it was funny, but I didn't want him to provoke Brian any more than he already had.

"Why are you even here?" I asked Brian. He turned to face me, and his ears went red. He opened his mouth and looked like a goldfish as he struggled to come up with an explanation.

"This place isn't real!" Brian insisted. "I made it up when I sent that stupid package away."

"What package?" I asked.

"You couldn't have made this place up," I heard a voice say, interrupting our conversation. I turned to look at where the voice was coming from.

"Nero said you would be a little surprised to suddenly be pulled into this place." The voice laughed lightly, and I saw a tall, dark-haired boy who looked barely a year older than me, leaning against the doorframe of what was clearly his bedroom. Now that the dust and clouds and wind had died down, I could make out the posters and pictures on the walls. There was an entire shelf stuffed with dog-eared books kept upright between trophies of various sizes.

"Nero?" I asked the boy stupidly. "How do you know Nero?"

"Hello, Jason," Nero's familiar voice said from behind me. I turned to look, but there was nothing. I turned back to face Rory, and he had a very knowing grin on his face. I turned back and Nero was there, suddenly visible.

"Have I told you how cool that looks when you just appear like that?" the boy said as Nero appeared behind me out of thin air.

"Boiling," Nero and I said at the same time, correcting him. I was grinning from ear to ear and held out my hand to Nero.

Nero returned my grin and carefully looked at my outstretched hand and said, "Remember the last time we did that?"

I laughed, "I don't think we have to worry about that this time, do you?"

We shook hands, and he pulled me in for a hug and a pat on the back. This time there wasn't a static shock, so I knew I wouldn't have any of his powers, but it was nice to see him all the same.

"How did you get out this time?" I asked.

Nero indicated the boy with a twitch of his head and smiled sadly, "Rory broke it."

I looked at Rory and held my hands up as if to say "so, explain yourself."

"Um, yeah, well, I dropped this diamond controller thing and accidentally kicked it." Rory paused and scrunched up his nose as he recounted the events, "And then my dog ate it."

I couldn't help but laugh at how silly it sounded, "Your dog ate it?" I was laughing so hard there were tears forming at the corners of my eyes.

"Well, yeah. It was an accident, though," Rory explained, looking sheepish.

"I'm starting to think that there was a reason that the controller was locked away in a glass case in an abandoned store," Anderson commented.

"Wait, how did it even get here?" Matt asked suddenly.

"You said it was safe at your place, right?" Emily asked.

"Yeah, I checked on it a few days ago. I'm the only one who goes up into the treehouse anyway," Matt said, looking very confused as he tried to retrace his steps.

"Where did you get the controller?" I asked.

"Dead Letter Office," Rory answered.

"The what?"

"It's where packages and letters go if they aren't addressed properly, or if we can't find who it belongs to."

"Ohhh," Greg and I said together.

"I still don't know why we're here," I said, drawing the attention back to why we were all suddenly standing in a stranger's bedroom on an island in the middle of the South Pacific Ocean.

Nero and Rory caught us up, and we all stared at them, mouths hanging open in disbelief.

"You sound like you've had a very busy day!" I said to Nero. "So what's the plan then? We have to get him back as soon as possible."

"We need the controller fixed, but in order to get the Ancient Wizards to actually help us, we have to become Battle Masters," Nero said.

"We have to renew our Battle Master title every season," Rory explained. "It's how they keep the games fair."

"So you have to go through all the effort again and again every time just to keep the title?" Greg asked.

"Exactly. If we want to keep the title, we have to practice and win every few months," Rory said.

"So when they say they serve only the Masters —"

"Yes, it means that they only help those who have been crowned Battle Royale Masters. In the week leading up to the main event, the winners are stripped from their titles," Rory said, running his hands through his head and sighing.

It took a few seconds for his meaning to become perfectly clear to me, and then I sighed with him. "Guys, it means we have to take part in this competition if we want to get Nero home."

"And get you home, too," Nero added.

"When is the next Battle Royale competition?" Brian asked impatiently.

"In three days."

Chapter 6: Switching Sides

"When it's time to sign up, we go to the Battle Arena in the center of the island," Rory explained. He knew everything about this game and was preparing us to win. I could see the spark in his eyes, and it was very similar to what Nero had in his whenever he let off a powerful move, or when he was charging up.

"When do we sign up?" Greg asked.

"Tomorrow at noon."

"What if we're late?"

"Then we don't play until next season," Rory said matter-of-factly.

"And when is that?" Brian asked, a strange light in his eyes.

"The next Battle Royale is in three months."

"Three months?!" Greg exclaimed.

"That's too long. We can't sit around and wait for the next one to come around. We have to get ready, and we have to do it now," I said, my voice rising a little in panic.

"Keep calm, everyone," Nero said, "we do what we have to. We will not wait that long because we will not miss our chance."

There was some uneasy chatter, but we all nodded. Nero was right. We were just going to have to make the best of this moment.

"One more thing," Rory said.

"What is it now?" Greg asked, his old habits rising to the surface again as he snapped at Rory. He looked ashamedly at his shoes and mumbled a "sorry" and let Rory continue.

"The only way to leave the island is to win."

"No pressure, then," Brian said sarcastically.

"Brian, please stop it. We have to work together. Can't you just try to be nicer?" Emily said. His lips formed a thin, angry line, but he didn't say anything more.

***

The next day, Brian peppered Rory with questions, following him around everywhere he went, asking which weapons did what and how they worked. Brian inspected everything he could get his hands on, asked about ammo capacity, what the knockout effects were, and how many hits each person could take from each individual weapon. I was unsure about having him on our team, but he did seem to be getting excited about the game.

I kept a close eye on him, but Rory seemed unbothered by all the questions. In fact, he seemed quite happy to share all his knowledge with the other boy and answered each and every question in as much detail as he could.

"Relax," Emily said, smiling at me, "he looks like he's very interested in the game, and he might actually like playing with us."

"I hope so," I said. I didn't really trust Brian, but I did want him to get along with everyone.

Brian continued his relentless assault well into the night and all through dinner. He only stopped to take big bites out of the fried chicken every few minutes.

We each took turns to listen in on Rory's little class. Brian barely acknowledged our presence, but it was nothing new, really.

When Brian finally stopped asking questions, we all turned to him expectantly.

"What," he said and shrugged his shoulders. "We should learn as much as we can, don't you agree?" With that he simply walked off with a spring in his step.

My eyes met Matt's, and we exchanged a meaningful look—Brian was up to something.

***

Rory offered up his room to Emily when it was finally bedtime, and the rest of us took the couches in the living room. He had grabbed a couple of sleeping bags and extra pillows. We all shared the space—more or less comfortably.

Nero was the only one who didn't need sleep, but I had noticed a slight dimming of the fire of his hair. To help keep Nero occupied while the rest of us slept, Rory set up an old laptop that Nero could use to keep himself entertained. I watched over his shoulder while Nero researched everything that he could think of. He even found and watched several videos showing the strategies the other teams had used, including old Battle Royale footage that showed what the Arena looked like.

Rory and the others had fallen asleep very quickly.

I kept glancing at Nero. He looked a little less bright the longer I spent looking at him. It reminded me of the last time he was in the human world. This time, though, Nero's powers seemed to be fading a lot faster than I remembered. It made me nervous.

"What happens if all your powers disappear, Nero?" I whispered as quietly as I could.

"I might get trapped here, or I might disappear completely."

"Or you could become mortal," I offered.

"Or that, yes. Without me, my world will also completely fall apart, Jason. There will be a disruption in the balance of power, and the bad guys will win. Let's not test that theory, okay?"

I nodded. I liked that Nero was here again and that I could talk to him in person, but I also knew that he missed his own world and his own friends.

"Then let's win," I said.

"Agreed."

***

There were nearly thirty kids about the same age in the Arena all around us, and the energy was electric! Everyone was talking excitedly, and I noticed there were smaller groups that were still trying to recruit members for their teams.

"There are always a few teams late to the party," Rory said with a smile. "It makes it fun when there are a lot more people in the Arena."

"How many teams are there usually?" Matt asked.

"Five or six," Rory shrugged. "Doesn't matter. The more the merrier."

I rolled my eyes at Rory and wandered around, looking at everyone that was gathered. I took in the sheer amount of people who would be participating in this season's Battle Royale.

"Emily, I want you to join me. We can be on our own team. Look around; there are a lot of people here we can make a team with," I heard Brian telling Emily. I wandered a little closer, my hands turned into fists.

"Brian, no. Jason and Matt, and the others, they're my friends, and I won't just abandon them," Emily said loudly.

We all turned to look at him.

"Come on –"

"I said no, Brian." She cut him off mid-sentence. "You're being a selfish jerk! I don't want to be friends with someone who is so mean all the time." Emily stormed past me.

"Wait, what are you doing, Brian? Where are you going?" I asked. I watched as Brian turned around and began leaving with a strange group of boys with green bandanas around their arms.

"Are you switching sides?" I asked angrily.

Brian grinned viciously, "I'm making my own team. I'm going to beat you guys and prove that I'm better."

"What?" we all shouted at the same time.

"What do you mean?" Emily asked. "You're supposed to be on our team. If you leave, they'll have to sign me up. I can't play. I don't know how to play."

There was a brief moment of hesitation, and then Brian replied in the meanest way possible, "You chose to be friends with Jason, so now you get to be on his stupid team."

"What's the matter with you, Brian?" Matt asked.

Brian turned around and faced his new team, "Let's go, boys. We don't need a bunch of losers." He and his group laughed menacingly, and then each of them bared their teeth at us like angry dogs before following Brian in the opposite direction.

"Well ain't that a pickle," Rory said.

Chapter 7: Game On!

"Before we get carried away with all the fancy weapons," Rory said, "we have to go over the rules."

"Rules? What rules?" Emily asked.

"There are always rules in these kinds of games," Matt said. "It's how they make sure people don't cheat."

"Like what? Don't punch someone in the nose?" Emily asked, looking at the rest of us through squinted eyes.

I laughed a little but stopped myself before I offended her. It wouldn't be nice of me to laugh at her just because she didn't understand. She was, after all, still learning.

"It can be like that, but here, it's more like how many people we can have on a team and what weapons we are allowed to use," Rory explained carefully.

He held out his hand and showed off a funny looking device on his wrist.

"What is that?" I asked. I had never seen something like it before, and since Rory hadn't had time to show us all the weapons that he had in storage, I assumed it must've been one of those. Nero used fire powers, and Crackle used close-range kung fu. Each of them had their own special powers, but none of them used weapons of any kind, so I couldn't even begin to guess at what it did.

"It's a smaller type of weapon we use," Rory said and aimed it at his bedroom wall. Immediately a gooey squelch erupted from it, and a spiral of green, sticky, smelly goop struck the wall.

"Urgh!" Greg exclaimed and stepped way from it.

"Like I have explained before, we don't hurt each other, but it sure does stink to get hit by this!" Rory laughed at all of our facial expressions, and we watched as it slowly started disappearing from the walls.

"That's so cool!" Anderson exclaimed. "When can we use those?"

"I've got a training course that my dad built for me out back," Rory said, grinning proudly as he pressed a button on his goop gun. It made a soft whir as if it was switching off.

"We can use the training course after dinner. My mom's homemade pie is the absolute best," Rory added.

"Won't it be too dark out?" Emily asked.

"Oh, no, not at all. My dad had some really bright lights installed, so I can practice for a little bit at night."

"Oh, like those floodlights at baseball games?" Anderson said.

Rory nodded.

"Wow, you must be so good at this then! We'll absolutely win with you on our team!" I said.

"I believe that a strong team will allow us to win the Battle Royale," Nero said calmly, nodding his head in agreement.

"But no one here has any real experience except you and Rory," Anderson said looking at Nero.

"Exactly," I agreed.

"That's not completely true," Rory said and pointed at Matt. "The tall one over there knows a thing or two."

Greg and Anderson snorted and looked at each other, "Matt doesn't really play that many games, though. None that we've ever seen."

It was my turn to snort, and I burst out laughing, "Matt's better at games than the two of you!"

Greg and Anderson pretended to be hurt by my comment, holding their hands over their hearts and pulling weird faces, "The betrayal! Oh!"

After a few seconds they laughed and grinned at us. We poked fun at each other once in a while, and it reminded me of how brothers picked on one another but still loved their siblings.

"We play a bunch of other games together when you guys can't make it over," I added and shrugged.

"Relax, everyone, it's not that complicated!" Matt said and he grinned. "Between the three of us, we can teach you all a thing or two, and we'll win for sure."

Dinner was a cheerful occasion. Rory's mom happily welcomed each of Rory's new friends and made sure that we all had enough to eat. She went above and beyond and even baked a second pie.

"Be good, Rory," his mom said and kissed him on the cheek. He awkwardly and half-heartedly pushed her away, blushing all the way to the top of his hair. "I will, mom."

Once the tables were cleared and the dishes were clean, Rory led us out back and unlocked the security gate to his training course. He locked the gate behind us again, "I don't want a little kid sneaking in here. If they didn't know what they were doing they could seriously get hurt."

"I also keep the weapons locked away unless I'm training, cleaning them, or making sure they haven't malfunctioned."

"They can malfunction?" Emily asked.

"Yeah, it happens from time to time," Rory explained as he carefully set each weapon side by side on a long counter in front of a target range. "The technology sometimes needs to be updated, or things can go seriously sideways."

"What happens if it, you know, malfunctions?" Greg asked cautiously and took a small step away from the weapons in front of him.

"Normally, it just misfires, but I heard a story that an ammo canister exploded in one of the janitor's hands and completely took off all of his fingers!"

"What?!" we all asked at the same time, staring at Rory in shock and horror.

"I'm just kidding, guys. It did explode, but it only made him smell like tuna for a week. The neighborhood cats wouldn't leave him alone." Rory laughed so hard there were tears forming in his eyes.

"Here, Emily," Rory said. He handed her the biggest Spinner he had hanging on the wall. "Relax. Seriously, I won't let anything happen to you."

"Oof, that's heavy," Emily said, and I reached out instinctively to help her hold it up.

"No, I have to get used to this stuff, Jason," Emily said with a little grumble in her tone.

"Hey, what did I do?" I asked and held up my hands.

"Nothing," she said, and shook her head. Emily suddenly looked sad, "You were right about Brian, Jason."

"You always try to see the best in people," I said. "It's not your fault he's a jerk."

Emily looked even more hurt by my words, so I just kept quiet. She lifted the weapon, and her arm shook a little, but she had a determined look on her face as she forced it to stop shaking.

"Sometimes we have to let them come to us," Nero advised, trying to make Emily feel better.

"I really thought we were maybe becoming friends," Emily said after a moment.

"I know," Matt answered for me, "but he has to choose to be our friend all by himself. I didn't make Greg and Anderson be friends with Jason." The other two boys nodded.

"And I didn't make them be friends with me, either," I offered. It only made Emily seem more sad, and I wished I hadn't said anything. I mentally slapped myself. I only seemed to be making things worse.

"Okay, so how does this work?" Emily asked, careful not to point it at any of us and ignoring my comment to focus on the task at hand.

We were all standing in Rory's backyard at the starting point of his Battle Royale training course. It was big enough that if you ran from one end to the other, you would be a little out of breath when you got to the other side. There were several targets that were all different sizes. Some were up in the air, and some were low to the ground to make it look like the target was crouching.

It was so cool that I couldn't stop smiling at all the different things Rory pointed out to us.

"There's a metal lever on the side, do you see it?" Rory directed. "Good, now pull it towards you, hold it for a few seconds while it charges, and then let go."

Emily did as he instructed, and a splurt of neon yellow liquid exploded from the end. It looked like a colorfully painted net as it flew through the air, splattering everything in its range. Her target was completely covered in the liquid and smelled faintly of old sneakers.

"Do you see the rope?" Rory asked. Just as he said it, I noticed the thin, wire-like rope attached to the weapon.

"Now, take the same lever that you used to charge it, and push it away from you."

This time the rope tightened, and a loud whir came from inside her weapon. Her target started being pulled towards her.

"Once the opponent is close to you and he's still conscious, you can smack them in the face with a Mini to knock them out. Other than the Big Betty, this is the best weapon to take out a person on the opposing team in one shot."

"Nice!" Greg and Emily said together.

"The problem is that you will need to have only one target. It works well on one person but not groups."

We spent the next few hours taking turns with the bigger weapons to see which of us could easily and successfully handle them. We laughed, shot each other, and just for fun, had a race through the obstacles to see who was the fastest. Rory offered advice to each of us in turn and praised Emily whenever she hit her target.

"You're doing great, Emily! Look at that! A little more practice and you can kick Jason's butt!"

Each weapon had a funny effect. Some froze you in place and encased you completely in ice. Another shot a ball of invisible energy at you that made your body go numb. One direct hit from close up with that weapon in the chest and you went down like a sack of potatoes.

It was fun getting to know Rory. He was the coolest guy I knew! That included Matt, Greg, and Anderson, too. He didn't seem bothered if he made a mistake or missed his target; he just kept going and made sure to hit it the next time. He only ever missed his target once.

And Nero was special and cool in his own way. Oh! I mean boiling! He hated being called "cool." Nero did have fire powers, after all, but he was right there with us, practicing using the weapons. He wouldn't be allowed to use his own powers in the Arena, so he made sure that he knew how to use what they were given.

"This is harder than I thought," Greg said as he missed his third shot in a row.

"Hey, we still have some time. You can do this, bud," I said and clapped him on the back.

***

"Listen up," Rory said while we were packing weapons back into their crates at the end of the night. We fell quiet immediately. He was so confident in everything that we automatically turned to him for leadership. "When the final gong goes, chaos is going to rain down on us from all directions."

"What do we do?" I asked, trying to be as brave as I possibly could be.

"We split up."

"Why –"

"Hold on, listen to the plan, boys. I believe I understand his strategy." Nero held up his hand and quieted Greg's interruption.

"We run in opposite directions," Rory continued. "They would expect us to separate, yes, but not like this. This is just the start though. The real plan will be different."

"I have seen how each team operates," Nero added. "They're not too smart for putting their team's strategies on the internet where anyone can find them."

"Wait, aren't Rory's strategies on there as well?" I asked, remembering that I saw a video clip of Rory leading his team.

Rory grinned, "Give me a little credit, Jason. Everything I do for this game is calculated, even the videos we upload to the archives."

"The archives are where past games are stored," Nero explained before anyone could ask. "It allows judges to make sure no one cheated, or a point isn't awarded to the wrong team if two people shoot the same opponent."

"The aim is to take out the strongest team first. That would be the blue team," Rory said.

"And how do we know that they're the strongest?"

"Because they were *my* team," Rory said proudly.

"Hey, don't get all weird on us. You're on *our* team now," Greg said, annoyed.

Rory laughed good-naturedly, "I know, Greg, don't worry."

"The good news is that you have me. I finish as Last Man Standing in nearly every single game that I compete in."

"What's the bad news?" Emily asked.

"Yeah, um, the bad news is that they know how I think. We've been competing together since we were ten," Rory admitted.

"So, we *shouldn't* split up?" I was confused. Rory just said that they wouldn't expect something like it, and then told us that the other teams knew how he played.

Rory and Nero exchanged glances and then turned to me, "Well, yes and no."

"So, we'll just have to surprise them, then. Do something that they don't think of," Greg said, jumping to his feet excitedly.

"How are we supposed to do something so completely original that they won't see it coming?"

Rory gave a sly little smirk, "By having someone else come up with plan B."

"What's plan B?" I asked.

"Plan B is how we win."

Rory leaned in closer, and he began to explain.

Chapter 8: It's a Battle Royale!

We approached the Battle Arena, all in a row. I was so nervous that I was trying not to throw up, so I distracted myself by listing off each of the weapons and what they did. I glanced at each of my friends. Nero didn't seem bothered at all. Then I realized why—he was used to fighting games. Facing off against an opponent wasn't new to him, and I was sure that he could master any of the weapons faster than any one of us could.

Rory was our team leader since he had the most experience. During our practice, he had let each of us practice a little with the weapons that he kept in his training room and also had each of us take a shot to the leg to see what it would feel like to be hit. Matt was the only one brave enough to be completely knocked out by that smelly goop-shooting blaster that Rory had demonstrated for us.

Rory had won nearly every season since he turned twelve. It was why his dad had helped him build the amazing obstacle and training course in his own backyard. It was a project that they had spent a lot of time on together, and Rory was always beaming with pride when he talked about his dad.

I glanced over at Emily, and she smiled reassuringly at me. I wondered how she would do. She had only watched us play Power Wolf Heroes and didn't seem too interested to attempt to play it herself, but she looked determined to do her very best.

She did try a few times, but one time Greg defeated her character so fast that there hadn't been time to learn how her Hero's skills worked. Greg apologized and promised to go easier on her.

Emily did try, but she just didn't seem to get as caught up in the thrill like we did. It was still okay because I liked having her there with me. She was excited when we won, even if she didn't understand the game very well.

Greg and Anderson were fidgeting with their bandanas or looking at their weapons as we approached the Arena. I could tell they were as nervous as I was.

Our group gathered at our team's point on the outside of the Arena. I couldn't even see the other side of the area it was so big, but I could hear various announcements being made over some kind of speaker system that sounded as though it was right in front of my face. The technology here was so advanced!

When all the teams were assembled, a loud cheer echoed through the Arena. I still couldn't see anyone, and I frowned at Rory in confusion.

"Wait, where are the people?" I asked.

"There are cameras that broadcast everything straight to our televisions in real time," Rory explained. He was getting worked up, jumping up and down in place and shaking himself out like a really big dog.

Matt looked calm like he was ready for anything that could happen today. It reminded me of the way he got when we played a shooter game at his house. My parents preferred to keep the violence to a minimum, so I only got to play the very bad ones (those were my parents' words, not mine) when I went to visit his house. He was really good at those games, always earning medals and badges, and he even taught me how to sneak up on our enemies before taking them out quietly.

"Is everyone ready?" Rory asked and stood up tall, his confidence boosting my own.

"Nope, but it's too late for that now," Greg muttered under his breath, and we all laughed awkwardly.

"OUR QUALIFYING TEAMS HAVE GATHERED AT THEIR STARTING POINTS!" the voice echoed through my brain. "THIRTY SECONDS ON THE CLOCK!" As the voice made its announcement, a countdown began in the background.

"Twenty."

"COMPETITORS, READY YOUR WEAPONS. WINNER TAKES HOME THE COVETED TITLE OF BATTLE ROYALE MASTER!"

"Ten seconds."

"GET READY FOLKS! IT'S ABOUT TO GET HAIRY OUT HERE!"

The invisible crowd cheered and roared their encouragement. I was being carried by their excitement and was slowly becoming less scared.

"You look nervous," Emily whispered to me as she lifted the heavy Splurt Spinner over her shoulder. Even though it was bigger than she was, she seemed to prefer it over the others. On her wrist I could see a very small device that looked exactly like a squirt gun. The little one sprayed the same old sweater smell into the eyes of anyone that got too close. It paired perfectly with the Spinner, and I smiled reassuringly at her.

"I'm excited, but I want us to win."

"I know we will win, Jason," Emily said, smiling.

"How do you know?"

"You're here, and I know you can do it."

I could feel my face burn a little hotter at her compliment. My heart was also beating faster for a whole different reason now.

At first there was nothing. No sound except silence as the final gong went. Then, we did as Rory had instructed—we split up.

Nero, Matt, and I were one group. The others had gone with Rory. Between Nero and Matt's Arena fighting experience, we had a pretty good chance at coming out whole on the other side.

We bolted in opposite directions and kept our heads down behind cover. At first I could hear nothing but my own breathing behind my face protection mask. Then, as if someone had turned the volume up on the world, sound exploded all around. It was soon after that that the sounds of people getting struck by beams, splurts, and sprays of various weapons echoed around us.

It was like nothing I had experienced before, but I found myself laughing as I dodged drops of unidentifiable liquids and bits of flying rock. I stuck close to Nero as we weaved through low walls, barrels, and other bits of cover. We were gunning straight for the blue team's starting point.

Rory's team was following the opposite curve of the Arena and was supposed to meet up with us there. His initial plan was to approach them from both sides. They wouldn't expect us to be stupid enough to walk right into their home base so soon.

Plan B, as it turned out, was exactly what the other teams did not expect. Matt was a whiz at strategizing, and since Brian left before anything serious had been discussed, we had managed to keep our plan a secret.

Rory had explained that in order for our plan to work, we had to bait the other teams into believing we were going to do exactly what they expected us to do—split up.

The trick was that we wouldn't stay separated.

It was pure genius.

We would split up at the start, taking as many of the groups out as fast as possible on our way to the blue team's starting location. Once we regrouped at our target point, we would scatter again, moving in teams of two with Rory flying solo, keeping our backs covered. We had to move as fast and as quietly as we could.

If we were in trouble, we would give one sharp whistle, and the whole group would reform and head straight to the source of the whistle. After the threat was dealt with, we would follow the plan again—split into two groups, then scatter into teams of two.

I walked at the back of the group, keeping an eye out for anyone sneaking up on us. I did a full, slow circle. Scanning carefully around me.

When I turned back, my entire team had wandered off. My eyes grew wide, and I dropped into an immediate crouch. My heart was hammering away in my chest, trying to break through my ribs.

I got separated!

I chose to run in the direction I had last seen them. I completely forgot that I could simply have whistled to get them to find me, but my brain was so full of panic that I blanked on the plan.

I kept running. I ducked into a smaller, windowless shack and hid behind the door. I checked my ammo count and reloaded. I was up to twelve shots again.

I heard movement outside and froze, feeling a little warm under my protective gear.

"I could have sworn I saw them go this way," I heard a voice say.

"I don't see anything," another replied.

"Well, it's not like the entire blue team decided to take naps together," the first voice said angrily. "They have to be here."

I readied my weapon and aimed it at the open doorway, waiting, barely breathing. As soon as one of the boys showed his face, I whistled as loud as I possibly could and fired my Old Zapper straight into the surprised face of my opponent.

He went down instantly, and I reloaded.

"What was that?!"

I aimed at the open doorway again, waiting.

I didn't have to wait long before I heard a scuffle outside and a yelp. The person fell to the ground. I clenched my teeth and kept my finger on the trigger, waiting for a new face to appear in the doorway.

A soft whistle sounded outside a second before Rory's face appeared in the doorway, "Keep up, will you?"

Chapter 9: Everything Gets a Little Crazy

I was getting better and better at handling my Old Zapper. I missed less now. I knocked out the last boy on the blue team by shooting him in his chest. He did a backflip as the blast hit him, and he went down in a puff of dust and sparks.

The Zapper sent a ball of electrical energy sparking towards the target and then stunned them upon contact. It was not as big as Emily's Spinner but not so small that I had to use multiple shots to take someone out. I was quite pleased with how comfortable I had become with this new weapon.

Once or twice throughout the game, I stopped to take a breath, looking around for my friends. I wanted to make sure they were all still safe. We needed to last as long as possible and gather many points from knocking out our opponents.

I heard a whistle and started heading in that direction. It was part of the plan. Hear a whistle, run towards it! I scanned the area as I ran, trying to keep my weapon and aim ready as I did so, but not really succeeding.

I slowed down to catch my breath and checked my surroundings again.

I couldn't see him, but I could hear Matt shouting orders to Greg and Anderson as they circled around the lone boy from the yellow team who was hiding in the ammo shack.

That meant two teams were down and three remained: ours, Brian's, and a team that managed to scrape together some extras for their group and made it in time. I had taken one of their team members out and noticed a purple bandana around his arm.

Before I had a chance to meet up with Matt's little group, I heard a low hum. Something in me froze, and I panicked. I dove behind the nearest cover and looked around frantically. The sound was only just familiar to me but –

There was a loud echoing boom, and I could feel the ground shake. Someone had found and used the Big Betty. I looked around in the air and saw the cloud of glitter. I knew that my guess was right. Rory had one or two in his storage room back at his house, but he refused to demonstrate that particular weapon. He said it was too dangerous to be used so close to other people's homes.

"It won't hurt the people, but it could break some windows," Rory had told us and laughed, explaining how he had gotten into trouble once for setting off a Big Betty inside his gym class at school.

"Mrs. Addy wasn't happy with me. I had to clean up all the glitter by myself every day after school. It took me a whole week!"

He did show us a video clip of someone using it in a previous match, and the result was amazing. The weapon itself looked like a fat loaf of bread. You stuck your hand in the one end, twisted a knob inside, and then threw the whole thing straight into the air above the area you wanted to target.

It took a few seconds, but we all watched in silence as it sailed across the sky with a low rumbling whistle, and then detonated three feet above the ground. The effect was colorful and was an instant knockout to whoever was caught in the blast.

There was glitter everywhere. Big Betty's explosion was incredibly loud and very, very sparkly. It took a few minutes for the sparkles and dust to settle, but once it had, the team that was caught in the blast was lying on the ground, out cold.

"Oh my goodness," Emily said, and we all cheered at how awesome it looked.

Rory had been right not to demonstrate it at his house.

The entire area was now covered in glitter, and I felt a little woozy from the after-effects of the blast. And I hadn't even been caught in it! The only way anyone would have survived that big explosion was if they were hiding inside a building with no doors or windows. Or if they were, like me, far enough away that they weren't in range of the Big Betty's knockout effect.

I waited just long enough for the echo to die down and the glitter to fall quietly to the ground like fresh snow before I ran in a crouch, creeping closer to the detonation site. The Big Betty had taken out Greg, Anderson, and two of the opposing teams 'members. It looked like someone misjudged the range of the weapon's knockout effect and ended up knocking themselves out in the process.

I saw the purple bandanas peeking through the glitter and mentally marked the four people off the list in my head. Greg and Anderson were the only ones from our team that had been knocked out so far, and Matt was nowhere to be found.

I skirted around the area, my heart beating so fast it felt as though it was going to pop out of my rib cage. I recognized Emily's soft whistle and felt both relieved and surprised that she had made it this far. I knew that everyone would try to keep her as safe as they could, but Emily would also try her best.

Chapter 10: Nero Loses?!

Matt and Emily had found Rory's unconscious form and whistled for us.

"Greg and Anderson are down, too," I said as Nero and I met up with them. Rory had taken a Mini Blaster to the back of the head. One of the boys on the Purple Team had managed to sneak up on him while he was peeking around the corner of the wooden shack he was using as cover. I saw a bright purple splat of paint on the back of his head as he snored away.

"What's the plan now?" Emily whispered as she pressed her back against the same wooden shack that Rory had used.

"Stick to the original plan and split up again?" I asked and saw panic enter Emily's eyes.

"I can't go out there all by myself," Emily said, her voice getting squeaky with panic.

"We're down to just the four of us. Brian's the only one from his team, and there's a few more guys from the Purple Team. I think we'll be better off if we stick together from here on out," Matt said as he loaded the last of his ammo into his Jello Splatter. The goop it fired stuck to the target like glue and would obscure your vision, making you an easy target to take out with a Mini Blaster or a Puff from close range. It also smelled like rotten eggs. It took a whole lot of hot showers to wash all that stink away.

"Brian's alone?" Emily asked.

Matt nodded and peeked around the corner to keep an eye out for anyone who would approach us.

"Coast is clear," he said.

"Right. Let's go."

We followed Matt's lead now that Rory had been taken out of the game. He was pretty good at coming up with a good plan on the fly. It was very easy to see why Rory would feel confident in his team and trust us to do our best.

The sounds of battle were beginning to come slower and less frequently, some further away I thought. That all made sense since so many players had been knocked out, but as much as the noise at the beginning made me nervous, now the quiet had the same effect.

The minutes that followed felt like hours. We creeped through the Arena slowly and as quietly as possible. Emily and I were guarding the rear while Matt and Nero were up front.

"Hey! Over here! I found two of them!"

Emily and I turned around at the same time. It was one of the guys from the purple team, his blaster aimed at us. He was attempting to call for backup, looking behind him to see if anyone else was coming.

Emily and I paused for only a very brief moment before we moved as if we were one body. We raised our weapons at the same time and fired. Both shots hit him—mine in his leg and Emily's in his chest. The combination of our attacks had knocked him out without him able to utter another sound.

Emily unhooked the rope from her Spinner and loaded the last of her shots, "I think this is all I have left. You'll have to cover me if we get cornered by more than one person."

She peeked around the corner, double-checking to see if his reinforcements were on their way, then turned back to me, smiling, "I don't see anyone else coming. I think –"

"Emily, behind you!" I shouted as a warning, but it was too late. Just as she turned to look behind her, the opponent got a shot on her. She flew back in a spiral of yellow liquid and rope. I dove behind the nearest cover and made myself as small as possible.

One of the boys on the purple team had hit Emily in the back with a Spinner of his own. His reinforcements had arrived. They were a little too late to save him, but their team scored a point. I was sweating beneath my protective gear and felt the dust and sand stick to my back, making me itch.

I had given my position away and saw Matt approach. I shook my head violently and mouthed, "Go!"

He had to get back to Nero. They could regroup and circle back around. They were the strongest players we had left, and I was pretty sure that Brian was still in the game. We couldn't afford to lose the strongest players, especially not now that we were so very close to winning.

I heard the purple guy sliding on the loose sand and fumble with his Spinner. He didn't seem to be as comfortable with the Spinner as Emily had been.

"How many of you are left?" I shouted. I wanted to distract him to make it difficult to reload. He definitely didn't seem to be very confident in his abilities, and I heard him mumble under his breath as he continued to struggle with the weapon.

"No-none of your business!" he called back.

I heard the faint whistle that summoned us together. It sounded like Matt was in distress.

I took a deep breath, jumped out from my hiding place, and fired my Old Zapper at him. His hand was still fumbling with the cartridge on the Spinner when his body went limp, and he fell against the broken cover, drooling as he slid down to the ground.

I stayed there just long enough to confirm that he was indeed unconscious and not just pretending. Then I ran as fast as I could in the direction of where I had heard the whistle coming from.

My whole body was tired from being so tense all the time. My muscles were sore and shaky. My legs burned when I crouched behind cover while I panted and tried to catch my breath.

"Matt!" I whispered loudly. It sounded funny to me, but I didn't want to shout and draw attention to myself. I had no idea who else was around, and I was almost out of ammo. I crept forward, checking behind every piece of cover.

I found Matt slumped against the wall of a small, empty metal shack. His weapon was jammed and his face covered in green slime. I sighed and checked again to see if there were any more ammo packs around somewhere.

Then I heard a second whistle and saw Nero. His weapon was out of ammo, and he flung it to the side. Our eyes met, and he gave me a confident wink, pulling one of the smaller Splatter-Crackers out of the strap on his hip.

It was a small weapon that looked like a feather duster, but when you whipped it at someone, it sprouted tentacles and wrapped around your target. Nero didn't get a chance to use it.

I heard the whine of a Snow Blaster as it charged for attack.

"No!" I shouted as loud as I could and bolted towards him. I knew I stood no chance of saving him, but I had to try.

It was just the two of us against them, and I couldn't do this on my own. I was reminded once again of the moment Matt, Greg, and Anderson had teamed up against me and were chasing me on their bicycles nearly every afternoon. I felt that same hollow, scared feeling in my stomach.

The giant ball of ice hit Nero square in the chest, and he stumbled backwards. I skidded to a halt in the open. I dropped my Mini Blaster on the ground in shock. Nero was my hero. He couldn't go down, not now. He was supposed to help me win! No one could defeat him!

But they had.

I watched as his entire body began turning blue. Ice crystals formed on his skin until he turned into one gigantic block of ice.

Chapter 11: Last Man Standing

A loud announcement echoed through the air in the Arena, "LOOK AT THAT, FOLKS! WE ARE DOWN TO JUST TWO PLAYERS, AND THE SCORES ARE EVENLY MATCHED! WHO WILL WALK AWAY AS THE BATTLE ROYALE MASTER?"

I skittered behind the nearest barrel and just sat there for a few seconds. Everything had happened so fast. Rory, Matt, and Nero were down. I was the last of my team.

"HOLD ON TO YOUR HATS, FOLKS, THERE'S A STORM COMIN'! WILL THEY DUKE IT OUT MANO-A-MANO OR GO THE SNEAKY ROUTE?"

I felt the sweat running down my back, and my throat was drier than the sand beneath my feet. It was Last Man Standing. Only one of us would walk away the winner.

"RED VERSUS GREEN! PLACE YOUR BETS, FOLKS! WHO WILL WIN?"

"Brian!" I shouted as the announcer's voice died down. The crowd's cheering fell quiet.

"What's the matter, Jason? Are you scared?" Brian shouted across the open space at me. He was right. I was scared, but I looked at where my friends all lay unconscious around me. They had all been knocked out. Either by Brian or by one of his evil teammates. I looked at Nero's body where he lay in the dirt, his mouth open. He let out a snort, and I jumped a little.

It was good to know that no one really got hurt. But with Nero down for the count, I had to win. I had to save us. My stomach dropped as I realized that our hope of getting home—of getting Nero home—was resting squarely on my shoulders.

If I lost to Brian, he would never let me forget it. In fact, I was pretty sure that this would be the one thing he would continue to throw back in my face and use to try to get Emily to be his friend again. If we lost, we would probably be stuck here forever.

"You're on the wrong team, Jason! You don't stand a chance against me," Brian screamed.

Would he stay here on Wipeout Island? Would he want to? He did really seem to enjoy the attention he got. He was also really good at the game. He knew which weapons worked well against which opponents, and it was easy to see why his team chose him as their leader.

"Face it, you're only going to end up losing to me anyway," Brian taunted.

I admired the way he played. He was so good! But it didn't take away the fact that he was still on the opposing team and wanted to defeat us just to prove that he was better. Maybe he would win and then refuse to help us get the controller fixed. The thought made me feel sick to my stomach.

"You're the one who chose the wrong side, Brian!" I said. "You chose to abandon your friends!"

His harsh laugh made me cringe. I remained silent this time. I waited for him to continue his shouting before I moved again. I needed him distracted just long enough so I could get closer to him. I had only one shot left, maybe two, and I had to make them count.

"You don't seriously believe that, do you?"

I could hear by his voice that he was coming closer. He wasn't even bothering with using the surrounding cover. He thought he had me. I grinned to myself, keeping my breathing steady and my footsteps light so that I could move as silently as possible. I crouched low and zipped around one of the half-walls, managing to position myself behind him.

"I don't want to be your *friend*, Jason! Nobody wants to be your friend!"

I bit my tongue and felt the anger his words brought out in me. Brian was such a jerk.

"I'm right, aren't I, Jason?" Brian taunted. I knew it wasn't really true, but it was hard when he spoke the things I thought about myself. I shook my head.

"You're wrong!" I darted from my hiding place and fired my Old Zapper at him. I missed, and my shot went wide! It struck the barrel and exploded in a ball of water and paint. I flinched as the mixture struck my face protection. I hastily wiped the paint away, smearing it a little.

"I just want you to disappear!" Brian shouted again. "Everything was fine until you showed up! Everything was fine until you became friends with Emily!"

I stepped out into the open and aimed my Old Zapper at him, but Brian had got what he wanted—an angry, thoughtless reaction from me.

Brian dove behind one of the broken walls on the battlefield and fired blindly at me. I tried to copy his movement and attempted to dive behind the nearest pile of broken bricks and rocks.

I was too slow!

The blast hit me like a superhuman punch, and I felt my body spin around from the force. I lost my balance but managed to stick my landing and scurried behind a wall. My arm was numb and tingly where Brian's blaster got me. I was lucky. A little to the left and I would have been knocked out.

There was no one but the two of us left in the Arena. Everyone else had been knocked out of the game. I couldn't let Brian win. It wasn't a matter of pride anymore, but a matter of urgency. Nero had to return to his home, and we had to return to ours.

I briefly remembered the time I had gotten lost in the grocery store when I was still a little kid, and my mom had started crying when she finally found me. I had felt bad because all I remembered was wanting a candy bar and going off to find one.

I couldn't let my friends get in trouble either. It was time to put an end to this.

I dove and rolled across the open space between us, aiming directly at Brian as I came to a stop.

I fired.

Chapter 12: Victory Royale

There was silence around me. Brian had taken the full force of my Old Zapper right to his face. I hadn't aimed at his head on purpose, but I panicked! I didn't really want to humiliate him, but we had to win, we just *had* to. I watched as he coughed and stumbled behind one of the smaller shacks. He only had one more hit left before he was out of the game. It meant we were evenly matched now.

I had rolled out of the way again as soon as my weapon had discharged. I kept running, trying to buy a little time while he got his bearings again.

"Why don't you just give up, Jason?" I heard Brian shout. I couldn't hear where his shout was coming from, but I risked a peek around the corner of some nearby cover. I still couldn't see where he was hiding, but I knew I couldn't sit around waiting for him to find me. He was clearly trying to get into my head and freak me out just like he did before.

I had to keep from replying, no matter what he said. Both Nero and Rory had taught me a few extra tips to help me survive in the Arena. I had kept asking questions, and they kept answering them even though it had gotten very late. I repeated their answers to myself over and over again in my head until I thought it was going to explode from all the information. It was like studying but a lot more fun, and instead of passing an exam, we would have to pass a team battle in a video game.

Remaining as quiet as possible when close to an opposing team member was one of the ones I remembered right now so that was what I did. I ignored everything that Brian shouted at me. It only stoked his fire and kept him screaming more hurtful things at me. This time, however, they didn't get to me.

I *knew* I had friends and that they *wanted* to be my friends. Even Emily had chosen to be my friend, even after the way I had used Naomi to make her feel jealous. Brian was wrong.

My Old Zapper was out of energy, so I laid it on the ground at my feet. I could feel a cold sweat drip down my back. I had only one weapon left, and it was one of the silliest things I had ever seen in my life.

I hesitated for a moment. I could run to the ammo shack and hope to grab something from one of the crates there, but it seemed very far away from where I was crouching awkwardly behind a barrel. My leg was still tingling where Brian's blaster got me. I knew if he managed to land another hit on me I would be knocked out, and he would be declared the winner.

I steadied my breathing and tried to remain calm.

The weapon I had left looked very much like a giant cotton swab with two oversized fluffy red balls on either end. It was called a Puff and covered your opponent in a cloud of colored powder that matched your team's colors.

A strange calm overtook me, and my mind cleared. This was my final boss battle, the one that I needed to win in order to beat the game. I could do this. I might not have super powers, but I had friends who believed in me.

I scanned the area around me, trying to find something I could use to my advantage. There were still splotches of various liquids drying in the sand and bits of broken wall and wood scattering the ground in every direction.

That was when I saw it. There was a small rock the size of a golf ball. It was against the rules to throw them at our opponents, but nothing stopped us from using them as a distraction. I relaxed a little and slowly peeked around the corner. Brian wasn't facing me but was still slowly moving in my direction—his weapon drawn.

With as much strength as I could summon, I threw the small rock as hard as I could in the opposite direction. It took a few seconds before I heard it clatter against the roof of the small metal shack, not even ten feet away from me.

I waited for a second more and leaned around my cover again, trying to see if he had taken the bait.

I saw an opening!

Brian had turned to face away from where I was hiding, toward the direction where the rock had clattered against the metal roof. He had his weapon at the ready and was crouched low to the ground.

His movements were precise and smooth, but also slower now. I admired how calm he appeared as he stopped to check behind other hiding spots. He approached the decoy.

I took a deep breath and rushed him, screaming as I did so. The wild look in my eyes must have startled him because Brian just stood there watching me run at him.

I slid on my knees in the sand and used all my strength to strike at his knees with the Puff. It made a satisfying 'thud,' and a cloud of red powder exploded around his knees.

Brian went down like a stack of bricks, crumpling in on himself. I quickly rose to my feet and stood over him. I could see that he was still conscious. His face was red as he glared up at me and made to shoot his blaster, aiming at my face.

With a quick poke, I shoved the other end of the Puff into his face. Again, it made a satisfying 'thud' and coated Brian in a layer of red powder. He blinked stupidly, coughed once, and his head rolled back and thumped into the sand, as he finally fell unconscious.

Chapter 13: Continue?

The crowd's response to the victory was broadcast into the Arena. It was so loud and so painful that I flinched, but I was also still hyper from all the excitement and the adrenaline pumping through my veins. I hopped in place, twirled my weapon in my hands, and then held it overhead. I could hear my heart beat in my ears, and I grinned widely. It was unbelievable! I had won!

I turned in a circle slowly, listening to the audience cheer over the speakers as I pumped my fist into the air. I soaked up their admiration. I kept turning in a circle, listening to their cheers. My eyes were now scanning around me for my friends and teammates. *We* had won!

After a few minutes, each and every person that had been knocked out in the last few rounds finally came to consciousness. Some of them giggled, and others had hiccups. It was one of the funny little side effects of the weapons that the competitors on Wipeout Island used. Emily coughed and a bubble of paint escaped from her lips, and then she laughed. It floated a foot above her head and popped, spilling a little bright pink paint on her head.

Nero's hair had turned a pale blue from the side effect of being hit by a Snow Blaster, and he looked incredibly unhappy about that. Greg and Anderson, who had been caught by the Big Betty, were still covered in heaps of glitter. They looked at each other with incredulous looks on their faces, and then burst out laughing, too. They high-fived and dusted themselves off.

Even on the opposite teams, people were waking up and laughing at their silly side effects. One player's ears had grown to three times their size and were bright green. My legs were still tingly from where Brian's blaster got me, and I wondered what my side effects would have been if he had managed to knock me out.

When everyone was treated and tended to, they each drifted to their respective groups in the very center of the Arena. The yellow and blue teams had lost in the first round. Nero, Rory, Matt, Greg, Anderson, Emily, and I were on the red team. Brian was the leader of the green team and now stood halfway between us and them, looking awkwardly at both teams.

"Jason!" Emily and Nero shouted happily as they surrounded me. All seven of us cheered and talked excitedly.

"Did you see that —"

"I know! I was taken out by a Big Betty! It was so awesome!" Anderson and Greg said at the same time. We were all chattering and gesturing, our arms flailing about as we described every moment of the battle as it happened.

I peeked through a small gap between someone's shoulder and another person's arm as they reached over one another in a big huddle. I could see the emotion on Brian's face. He wasn't sure what to do or who to side with. His team looked miffed that he had lost, but they didn't really seem to blame him. He did, after all, make it to the final round, even if he didn't manage to secure a win for the green team.

Brian's gaze met mine, and I could tell he really just wanted to celebrate something with someone. For a brief moment I could feel my old dislike for him rise inside me, but then I thought about how lonely it must be for him. I knew I was that lonely when I didn't have any friends.

"Hey guys, there's something I have to do real quick," I said distractedly and gently extracted myself from all the hugs and handshakes and friendly noogies I was receiving from all my friends. I walked to where Brian stood and held out my hand to him.

"What are you doing?" he asked, his voice sharp and his face scrunched up in confusion as he stared at it.

"It's called a handshake, duh," I said and poked my hand at him again. "I want to congratulate you on a good game. I really had fun today and you know, you're really good at it, too."

Brian took his hand from his pocket and slowly reached out and grabbed mine. He shook mine hesitantly, and when he saw I was really just being nice, he shook it with more energy and trust.

I smiled at him, and he smiled back, "I had fun, too."

"Um, listen, Jason. I'm sorry for being such a jerk." Brian's face was red with shame, and he didn't look me directly in the eyes.

"We're better off as friends, don't you agree?" I said, and slapped him on the shoulder playfully.

"I think so, too." Brian grinned and put his hand on my shoulder in return.

"You should say goodbye to your team," I said and jerked my head at the group of boys that were curiously looking at our conversation.

"Why?" Brian asked, looking angry again.

"Don't you want to come home with us?" I looked back at Emily, and all my friends looked back at Brian, "I'm sure if you apologize to Emily as well, she'll forgive you. She's a really good person."

"Are you sure?" Brian frowned.

"Yes. Come with us. We can play games together back home. We always need an extra person if someone has to go home early," I said and returned to my group. We were finally going home.

***

"Will you help us now?" I asked, carefully holding the controller out to the Wizard. His wrinkled hand appeared from the folds of the long sleeves of his robe, and he wrapped his long, thin fingers around the mangled plastic. He nodded once, and the controller disappeared from view beneath all the dark blue fabric.

The Wizard said nothing as he turned and disappeared into the back room of his little house. His mysterious friend followed after him just as quietly. He disappeared through the same curtained doorway.

"Do you think they can fix it?" I asked Rory.

"Of course, they're the oldest and wisest of anyone on Wipeout Island," Rory said, holding his arms behind his head very casually. He looked so cool standing like that, almost as if he practiced striking a pose in the mirror.

"We'll get you home soon," Nero said.

"And you," I said.

"I'll be able to return you to the same place that my summoning powers took you from," Nero said, looking at his reflection in the shiny surfaces of the Wizards' contraptions that littered their small countertop. His hair was back to normal now, but it didn't stop him from making sure. He ran his fingers through his red hair.

"My powers are almost completely gone now," he said with concern.

"How long do you think we've been away?" Emily asked, looking worried. "I didn't say goodbye to my parents."

Nero looked deep in thought for a moment and then said, "Time doesn't act differently here than in your world, so I would say about two days."

"Oh man, my parents are going to be so mad," Greg said, scrunching his face up.

"I wish I could move you back to the exact time I took you from, but my powers don't work that way, even at full strength." Nero touched Greg's arm reassuringly, "You have each other, young Greg. You can find a way to fix any problem as long as you have each other."

The Wizard came back with the controller. It looked good as new, with lightning sparking inside the see-through diamond case. We all sighed with relief, but no one was as glad as I was to see it finally fixed. Nero could go home to his own world, and get back to saving his own people.

We all rushed back to Rory's place. Brian was trailing behind, but no longer making mean comments.

It was finally time to head home. We were all standing awkwardly in a small circle in Rory's room. A tense but excited energy sparked through us like the lightning sparked through the controller. Rory stood with the connector in his hand, waiting for us to say our goodbyes.

"It has been nice to fight alongside you, Jason," Nero said.

"I really wish you could stay," I said.

"I know, my friend." Nero smiled sadly at all of us as we stood around the gaming console that was ready to take him back to his world in Power Wolf Heroes.

I held up my fist and aimed it at Nero. He looked puzzled from it back to me, "What are you doing now, Jason?"

"It's a fist-bump."

"Like this," Rory said and bumped my fist. "It's a cool way of greeting between friends."

"I understand," Nero said and touched his fist to mine. I grinned at him.

"You were amazing out there, everyone. It makes me happy that you all grew into such wonderful people and even better friends."

"Yeah. Yeah, we are," I agreed and looked at each of my friends in turn, even at Brian who stood awkwardly to the side as we all said our goodbyes to Nero.

***

"Jason!" my mom shouted as she threw her arms around me, crushing the bones in my body in happiness. There were tears in her eyes, and I could see the relief on my dad's face who was standing behind her.

"Where have you been, young man?" he asked sternly, although I could tell it was only because he had been so worried.

"When did you get here?" I stammered.

"This morning. Jason, Mrs. Thandie told us she hadn't seen you since Friday at lunch with your friends."

"Friday?" Anderson asked from behind me.

"Where have you *all* been? We looked through the whole house," Mr. Ash said, raising his voice.

"We, uh –" I didn't want to lie to them, but I really didn't think they would believe me if I told them that we were players in a Battle Royale, and in order to get home we had to win.

"Hello, Mrs. Ash, Mr. Ash," Matt said as all six of us piled into the kitchen. Nero had teleported us out just as Rory plugged the controller into the console. It was the only way Nero could boost his strength enough to send us home. His powers had drained away faster than they had the last time, and he hadn't had enough juice to whirlwind each of us back into our own houses.

"Hello, Matthew," my mom replied cheerily, never forgetting her manners, "it's so nice to see you again." Her smile only lasted a brief moment before she remembered that she was upset with us. My dad looked at us with a stern expression on his face and grumbled a "hello."

"Well young man, where were you?" he turned to me.

"Answer your father, Jason. We were worried sick!"

"They were with me, Mr. Ash," Brian said quietly and stepped forward. "I told them that I had the new Game Master 2000. I wanted them to play with me, and I guess in the rush we forgot to leave a note."

GAME OVER

REMATCH?

YES? ⬅   NO?

Hi Gamers!

Thank you for reading my book! It really means the world to me. If you enjoy this book, then I'd like to ask you for a favor. Would you be kind enough to leave an honest review on Amazon? It'd be greatly appreciated and help other gamers with their reading skills! I read EVERY review I receive and each one helps me become the best writer I can be!

Have fun!

Dan Ashcraft

Free Bonus!

Want to get a FREE 'A Video Game Story: Another Magical Controller?!' Ebook? This is an awesome short story that is a part of the 'A Video Game Story' world!

GO TO THIS LINK FOR YOUR FREE 'A VIDEO GAME STORY' EBOOK! -

bit.ly/avideogamestory

Enjoy!

www.ingramcontent.com/pod-product-compliance
Lightning Source LLC
Chambersburg PA
CBHW081402070526
44583CB00020B/2646